GARHWAL & KUMAON

Pindari Glacier

GARHWAL & KUMAON

A Guide for Trekkers and Tourists

by
K.P.Sharma

CICERONE PRESS
MILNTHORPE, CUMBRIA

© K.P. Sharma 1998
ISBN 1 85284 264 4
A catalogue record for this book is available from the British Library.

Photographs by the author
except where otherwise credited

CONTENTS

PREFACE

This guidebook is the result of six years' effort. It would not have seen the light of the day but for the active guidance received from my two friends Robert Howard, a freelance photo-journalist, and Michael Jones, a naturalist, both from Leicester in the UK. Michael Jones also introduced me to Walt Unsworth, Editorial Director of Cicerone Press, who agreed to publish this book. Robert has very kindly helped to write the sections What to Take and Health and Fitness. The book is primarily meant for overseas visitors on the lookout for exotic new destinations with a unique cultural experience. It will also help Adventure Tour companies to promote a little-known region of today, destined to become a "tourist boom" of tomorrow. I have endeavoured to include practical information on what a foreign visitor may need to know to help him enjoy his holiday.

Some distinguished writers, including my friend Kedar Singh Fonia, have written very informative books on tourism in Uttarakhand. I have been inspired by these books, and by my own trekking experience of Garhwal and Kumaon over a period of nearly four decades, to produce a guidebook with as much information as possible. While collecting or verifying details, I have referred to the *Gazetteer of Garhwal Himalaya* by H.G. Walton, *Uttarakhand* by K.S. Fonia and *Garhwal Ka Itihas* by Pt. Harikrishana Raturi. Information on procedure for mountaineering expeditions was obtained from the Indian Mountaineering Foundation. Nidhish Sharma, who has organised treks for Europeans since 1983, has shared valuable information with me. My colleagues Anita Shah and Sangeeta Rawat typed the manuscript several times, working late in the office. Michael Dafydd Jones has contributed the section on Flora and Fauna, and Roy Church, a keen fisherman and fan of the Indian Himalaya, has written the section on fishing. Vivek Doval helped to tie up several loose ends, and many photographer friends have contributed pictures. I am grateful to all of them and to others who were directly or indirectly associated with the birth of this book.

It gives me great pleasure to record my affection for my

granddaughters Shubhangi, Srishti and Smriti who will be able to read and appreciate this book in about 15 years, probably when I am no longer in this world. These tiny tots, by their wits and affection, have given me the energy and relaxation of mind to write the book.

This book is going to press as the creation of a separate State of Uttarakhand, constituting all the twelve hill districts of Uttar Pradesh covered in this guide, is round the corner. People have campaigned peacefully for over three years for a separate state to ensure better administration and to accelerate the pace of socioeconomic development in the hill region of U.P. I dedicate this guidebook to the memory of those gallant sons and daughters of Uttarakhand who helped in this, often in difficult circumstances.

I hope this book will motivate readers to experience an adventure holiday to this part of the Himalaya while it is still quiet, with clean campsites. I would be grateful to receive any feedback from readers to help me update any subsequent edition. The views expressed in this book are my own. It would not be unusual for any reader to differ with my views but I would not like to enter into any arguments about it.

K.P. Sharma, 1998

PART 1
Introduction

Garhwal and Kumaon divisions, known together as Uttarakhand, are the mountain regions of Uttar Pradesh in India with Nepal in the east, and Tibet in the north. An extension of the southern border of Nepal, drawn in a south-east to north-west direction through Uttar Pradesh, would roughly define the southern boundary of Uttarakhand: Himachal Pradesh is on its west. For geographical purposes the area can be subdivided into five regions: The Terai (plains), Lower hilly region, Upper hilly region, High altitude region, and Upper high altitude region. Uttarakhand is situated almost at the centre of the great Himalayan chain with over 250 peaks above 5500m high culminating with Mt. Nandadevi (7916m), the highest in the region.

It consists of a succession of steep mountain ridges divided from each other by deep glens. The valleys occasionally open out, but usually are narrow and precipitous. A traveller entering Garhwal from Kumaon in the east is at once struck with the more rugged character of the scenery which is in striking contrast to the milder aspect of the Kumaon hills which are more in the shape of a plate.

Garhwal is drained entirely by the Ganga (Ganges), Yamuna and Bhilangna rivers and their affluents. In proper terms, the name Ganga is applied to the river formed at the junction of Alaknanda and Bhagirathi at Devprayag. According to legend, the Ganga descended from heaven at Gangotri as a result of meditation by King Bhagirath for salvation of his ancestors who died there from the curse of a sage for being disturbed from deep meditation. Factually Bhagirathi is Ganga, the holy river. Hindus call Ganga, out of reverence, 'Ganga Ji'. The word *Ji* is to add respect, like 'Mr'. The British, perhaps, could not pronounce Gangaji properly and called it Ganges by which name it is known today by most people. Garhwali and Kumaoni, being very religious people, have suffixed the name *ganga*, meaning holy, to several other rivers and streams, such as Vishnu Ganga, Dhauli Ganga etc. It is in this context that Alaknanda is also called Gangaji by religious people because it

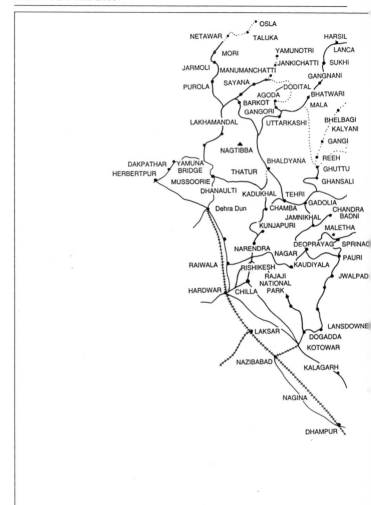

GARHWAL & KUMAON (UTTARAKHAND)

passes through the holy shrine of Badrinath. Kumaon is drained by the Ram Ganga, Gori Ganga and Pinder rivers. The first two rivers drain the eastern and southern flanks of the Nandadevi sanctuary. The Pinder river originates from Pindari glacier, below trails passing at 6100m. Much of the area is forested from the lower hilly to upper hilly region. The main trees are pine, himalayan oak, fern, spruce, deodar, kail and rhododendron.

Climate in Uttarakhand varies a great deal. It ranges from tropical heat to severe cold. In river valleys the day temperature rarely falls below 20°C and often exceeds 32°C in the shade during the summer months. In the winter the valleys are generally shrouded in mist during the night and morning, resulting in intense damp and cold. The climatic conditions of the Bhabar-Ramnagar belt at the foot of the hills are similar to those in the plains. In the south, snow rarely falls below 1500m though in the north it sometimes falls even at 1200m. During the winter months the snow line descends to about 2700m. In July-August it rises to about 5400m. By and large, above 1900m the climate is cool throughout. There are broadly five seasons: spring in March-April, summer in May-June, rainy season July to mid-September, autumn in October-mid-November, and winter from November to February. During May local thunder showers are frequent, often accompanied by heavy hail. These summer showers rarely occur at night and usually last for 15 minutes to an hour. Average rainfall in Uttarakhand would be about 95 to 250cm. It is very heavy during July-August. The pattern of rainfall at the beginning and end of the monsoon is of short duration, with heavy rain once or twice a day. In July-August heavy rain may sometimes continue a whole day and night without much of a break, otherwise it does stop for a few hours every day. In Uttarakhand the rain usually breaks earlier than in the plains, heavy showers apparently of local origin accompanied by northerly and westerly winds. The scouring action of these early showers on the dried up and pulverous soil is very great, and the damage done by erosion, in spite of comparatively less rain, is usually much greater than at any other time of the year. There are landslides, and piles of boulders and dry course-sand washed down from the hillside is brought down by the first showers, blocking roads at several places.

It is a delightful country of unsurpassed beauty with its soaring peaks, glistening glaciers, forested hills, flower-strewn meadows, butterflies, birds, wildlife and the very friendly, simple people. It is full of religious myths, abode of gods, saints and sages. It is one of the remotest, unspoilt and relatively unexplored regions and yet easily accessible.

Four of the most sacred shrines - Yamunotri, Gangotri, Badrinath and Kedarnath - are visited by thousands of pilgrims every day during the season. There came initially only the devout in search of religious salvation and then during British rule came the mountain lovers and adventure seekers. Visitors find peace and tranquillity in the several wilderness trails through dense forest which lead to lush, verdant valleys carpeted with alpine flowers in the season. There is nothing that one cannot discover in Uttarakhand. The devotionally adorned temples with their pinnacles soaring into cosmic blue tend to heighten in mankind an ecstatic sense of complete surrender to the Absolute Being, and the blue-emerald lakes, majestic waterfalls, meandering rivers, undulating meadows, rich thick forest, incredible mountains, and interesting villagers are a glorious combination. Having been closed to explorations and treks for about three decades from the early 1950s, Uttarakhand is gradually opening its doors to adventure lovers.

KEY TO MAPS

ROAD	———	RIVER	〰〰〰
TRAIN	+++++++	TOWN	●
TREKKING ROUTE	· · · · · · ·		

History and Society

Garhwal and Kumaon combined were believed to have come under the Katyuri dynasty in AD 850-1050. The kingdom became disintegrated in AD 1300 with the Katyuri rulers forming a separate state of Kumaon. Garhwal was divided into several small principalities. These were unified in AD 1500 into one kingdom under the rule of the Panwar dynasty. After Katuri, the Chand dynasty ruled over Kumaon till the eighteenth century. The Gorkhas ruled over Kumaon from 1790 to 1815 when they were defeated by the British East India Company and British rule was set up there. Kumaon has an area of 21,035sq km.

The name Kumaon is derived from a Sanskrit word *Koorm*, meaning tortoise. It is believed that the second incarnation of Lord Vishnu visited the earth by appearing on a hill near Champawat in Pithoragarh district in the form of a tortoise. The hill was thus named Koorm and the entire area came to be called Koormanchal. With the passage of time it became Kumu and in the sixteenth century the Chand rulers named it Kumaon. The land of Jim Corbett's legendary exploits lies due east of Garhwal from which it is separated by the eastern and southern flanks of the Nandadevi sanctuary leading down along the valley of Ramganga. Whereas Garhwal abounds in pilgrim centres and the mountains of the Ganga-Yamuna basin, Kumaon is wrapped in the scenic charm of hill stations. Till the opening of proper roads, trekkers and mountaineers bound for central Garhwal commenced the long trek at Ranikhet in Kumaon to enter Garhwal at Gwaldom. In the extreme west are the valleys of the Lassar Yankti, the Dharamganga and Kuthi Yankti rivers, bordering Tibet on the route to Kailash-Mansarovar via Lipulekh pass and the Api-Nampa peaks of Nepal separated from Kumaon by the Kali river. The original inhabitants of Kumaon are said to be Kols.

Broadly, Garhwal is bound by Yamuna in the west and the Ganga (Bhagirathi) in the east. The Borasu and Lamkhaga passes lead from Garhwal (now Uttarkashi district) to Kinnaur in Himachal Pradesh, across the western perimeter of the region which runs

14

along the Tons-Sutlej watershed. The eastern perimeter of Garhwal runs along the outer rim of Nandadevi Sanctuary down to Alaknanda-Pinder confluence in Chamoli district. Some of the country's most enduring rivers and many of the most spectacular valleys are situated here.

In the ancient Hindu religious books called Puranas, Garhwal is called Kenderkhand. Hundreds of years ago there lived several chieftains and landlords who ruled over their estates from forts (*Garh*) built on hilltops. There were 52 such forts which provided security and also served as watch towers. Thus the name Garhwal meaning 'of forts'. Some of the forts had underground paths made right down to the river below to draw water. Occasionally one finds rusty, broken sword-like objects, shaped stones, etc. in some of the ruined forts. It is said that a brave King Ajay Pal defeated the chieftains of all the 52 forts and renamed Kedarkhand as Garhwal during 1500-1515.

Between 1803 and 1815 Gorkhas from Nepal attacked Garhwal regularly. They were very cruel and tortured people for money. The killer of a cow or bullock was given a death sentence because such a killing was considered a sin, but they did not consider killing a human being as a sin. If anyone could not pay a fine, their entire family were made slaves. Anyone who had money could buy and sell slaves at Rs10-150 each. Thousands of people aged 3 to 30 were taken to Nepal as slaves. People were mortally afraid of them and would leave their houses to hide in forests for several months. In 1814 King Pradumn Shah requested the British East India Company for military assistance to drive out the Gorkhas. On successful completion of the operation a part of Garhwal called pauri Garhwal and Dehra Dun were gifted away to the British in recognition of their assistance.

The aboriginal inhabitants of Uttarakhand are believed to be the Shudras, or 'untouchables'. Brahmins and Rajputs, who constitute the major landowners in the area, are believed to have immigrated in the eighth century and later from places as far as South India, Bengal, Central India, Rajasthan, Himachal Pradesh and Kashmir. They were probably the defeated people from the Aryan invasions or runaway settlers as a result of wars over many years in the plains, who took refuge in the hills. It is said that some of the Brahmins were invited to become priests and cooks of the then King Kanakpal in the ninth century, and his successors. These Brahmins came and settled with their close relatives.

They are called Sarula Brahmins and consider themselves superior to other Brahmins, commonly known as Gangaris. The Brahmins and Rajputs were later divided into subcasts which mostly correlated to the village they originally lived in, after immigration.

A few examples of the casts so derived in Garhwal are given below:

Present Cast	Cast Before Immigration	Immigrated From	Year Of Immigration	Village
Dangwal	Dravid	Karnataka	8th c.	Dangwal
Painuli	Gaur	South India	12th c.	Panyal
Dhaundiyal	Gaur	Rajasthan	16th c.	Dhaund
Kainthola	Bhatt	Gujrat	15th c.	Kaintholi
Kothari	Shukla	Bengal	16th c.	Kothar
Panthri	Saraswat	Punjab	15th c.	Panthar
Chamoli	Dravid	Karnataka	8th c.	Chamoli
Parmar	Parmar	Gujrat	8th c.	Not known
Thapliyal	-	-	8th c.	Thapli
Bahuguna	Adyagaur	Bengal	8th c.	Bugani
Patwal Gosain	-	Delhi	11th c.	Pata

Rajputs mostly use the surnames Bisht, Negi, Rawat, Bhandri, and Gosain. Actually, these are not casts but titles bestowed by the kings of Garhwal. Bisht and Negi are civil titles; Bhandri was controller of finances or stores; Rawat and Gosain were military titles. Later on these titles became hereditary. Today, you will find people in Uttarakhand from all parts of India, settled in towns.

By and large three casts - Brahmin, Rajput and Shudras - predominated in the rural areas. It is important to mention here that after the independence of India in 1947, the social evil of practising untouchability with Shudras and cast system has been legally done away with.

PEOPLE

The Bhotiyas are of four classes, Marchhas, Tolchas, Jads and Juharies, inhabiting the Mana, Niti, Nilang and Johar valleys respectively. They are Hindus who for several generations had been doing flourishing trade with Tibet via the high passes. Ancestors of the present-day Bhotiyas must have married Tibetan women and therefore have Mongolian features. They are, however, not by any means identical to Tibetans. Unfortunately, with the change in political set-up in Tibet, business between the Bhotiyas of Uttarakhand and Tibet was discontinued in 1960. They have been forced to find an alternative source of income. In the early days the chief exports from India to Tibet via the passes and carried on the back of sheep, goats and mules used to be food grains, onions, clothes, sugar, tobacco, spices and dried fruits against the import of salt, borax, ponies, yaks, goats, sheep, dogs, wool, woollen goods and yak tails. Indian money was freely accepted. A special breed of sheep or goat carries a 6-8kg load packed in a sack called a phancha which is balanced on the back and fastened around the fore and hind legs. During winter months the Bhotiyas transport their merchandise to the market centres. They begin their day's journey before 4am and it is always over by 9 or 10am in all weathers. This gives them time to graze their flocks and to sell their merchandise to the villagers en route.

The present political leaders in India and China are working hard to improve relations between the two countries and one trade route between Uttarakhand and Tibet via Taklakot has been opened. Arrangements already exist between India and China to allow groups of Indian pilgrims to visit Kailash-Mansarovar during summer.

The people have in some ways remained somewhat submissive and aloof for centuries. Prior to the nineteenth century the several landlords and chieftains ruled without passing on any socio-economic benefits to the people. These rulers fought between themselves and attracted the attention of outside forces. Those who immigrated to Uttarakhand included those who came on pilgrimage or were specially recruited and charmed by its peace and serenity, and decided to settle here. There were also fugitives and culprits from outside who found the hills of Uttarakhand a safe sanctuary to live in peace. The last categories were the soldiers and warriors who came to invade and decided to settle here. All this perhaps resulted in lack of understanding for each other, lack of faith and insecurity. Then came the invasion of Gorkhas, which virtually crippled their spirits. They accepted orders from those wielding authority. When the British took over the reins of administration, life in Utterakhand was in such a sorry state of affairs that they introduced a 'Kuli Bardayash' (free labour) system under which villagers were compulsorily employed as porters to carry the luggage of government officials, without any payment, from one village to another. On top of this the villagers had to provide vegetables, milk, etc. free of cost to the touring officials. It must go to the credit of the British educational system that some educated personalities of Uttarakhand organised a successful campaign against this evil practice and the British rulers had to give it up in 1920.

Village women from Uttarakhand are very fond of singing, either individually or collectively, while collecting grass and firewood, while working in the fields and at certain social gatherings. The songs, composed by themselves, are about love, pain, sorrow, scandal, romance, ridiculing certain customs, recounting historical events and bravery in battle, and so on. There are some competitive group songs, composed instantaneously as the competition is going on, whereby the last line of the song sung by the first group is either repeated or replied to by the second group and a new verse is added to it. It is carried on and on till one party gives up by not being able to add anything within a few seconds. Such group songs are usually sung at fairs and festivals. There are certain songs and dances which are performed at night. In some dances men and women both participate but these are individual village affairs and not open to everyone.

FOLKLORE
The folklore of Kumaon and Garhwal represents a rich cultural heritage. Their folk songs are based on nature, love, cultivation of crops, describing gods and goddesses, warriors etc. They are accompanied by simple musical instruments like the Hurki, flute, Dhol and Nagaras. Some of the folk songs are sung along with dances which are usually performed in a circle. Some dances are

Kumaon dance

performed only by men, in others women participate. Their co-ordination of arm and foot movements is spectacular. The folk art reflects religious motifs. The pictures are drawn either on the walls or paper in natural colours made from rice and wheat flour. One such folk art is Alpna, usually found in Kumaon at the entrance to a house, wall or prayer room and on surfaces where pots of water and baskets of flowers for offering prayers are kept. It is drawn very artistically with rice paste mixed in coloured (usually red) clay by finger, palm or an improvised brush consisting of some cotton tied to a stick.

VILLAGE LIFE

Many of the villagers own cattle. While cows and buffalo provide a somewhat meagre milk supply, bullocks are used to plough fields. In the lower and upper hilly region goats and sheeps are reared. Mules and ponies are used to transport goods in villages not connected by roads.

Much of the land available for cultivation is in terraced form or sloped. This makes cultivation difficult because of soil erosion. New methods of farming are still unheard of in the hills and irrigation of the land is difficult owing to the mountainous nature of the area. Most landowners are dependent on rainfall. The main crops in winter are rice, millet, pulses and soyabean, and in summer wheat, barley, sweetcorn, oil seeds and pulses. People have now taken to growing vegetables and fruit, mostly apples and oranges, to produce cash crops. In villages above 2000m Ramdana or Chuwa (*Amaranthus paniculatus*), buckwheat, potatoes and beans grow in large quantities and are treated as commercial crops.

The general economic condition of people in towns and religious centres is somewhat better than those living in the country areas. The shopkeepers and tradesmen earn their living through tourism and other commercial activities. The government has introduced some welfare and developmental schemes in villages to promote education, self-employment, road-building, supply of water and electricity etc. The execution of the schemes is faulty, however, and the benefits are squandered by middle men and officials. Better execution of the schemes would have reduced the alarming exodus of educated people from the villages to the comforts of cities.

Some areas of Uttarakhand give an impression of being overcrowded. This is because a large portion of the land is covered by perpetual snows, some parts are too precipitous for cultivation, some lie above the limits of profitable cultivation, and some are reserved for pastures and forest. Villagers have the proprietory and cultivating rights over land in their own hands. In this capacity they are known as Zamindars, or farmers. The hill farmers cannot grow enough main staple grain, such as rice and wheat, to sell. On the contrary they frequently have to buy it from the market. The land is treated as joint family property and is subdivided between brothers down the generations. Unfortunately a system of primogeniture does not exist in India. This has often led to massive fragmentation of originally sizable land holdings, which in turn has resulted in an exodus of manpower in search of employment. Thus men tend to emigrate to the towns and cities, leaving their wives and children at home to manage the land.

The exodus of manpower places a considerable burden on the womenfolk left behind at home. Most of them are left in sole charge with their menfolk returning for only 4-5 weeks each year. When the

Ralam villagers

men do return home, they do not feel inclined to do agricultural or domestic work. Customarily women work very hard in the villages. They do nearly all the field work except the actual ploughing. They sow, weed and reap (in which the menfolk help, but not regularly), carry fuel and fodder from the neighbouring hills or wherever available, do all the cooking, washing, laundry, grinding, milking, babycare, bringing water from the village spring, etc. They are not, however, permitted to work as porters, domestic servants, or road builders. Years ago it was rare for any women to have any formal education. Since 1947 female education has considerably improved, though in remote villages it is somewhat neglected. Most women on completion of their education (or even postgraduates) settle down in marriage to respect the social practice. Few take to the teaching profession or office work, though some women from Uttarakhand have become successful journalists, scientists, doctors and mountaineers.

People from Uttarakhand are very self-respecting to the extent of being illogical at times. They are as a rule trustworthy, sober and good tempered, though childishly suspicious and impatient of restraint. By and large they are litigious, envious of their neighbour's good fortune and hesitant to do away with age-old obsolete social practices. The more the various development and educational schemes progress towards the villages, the more they tend to claim their rights, ignoring their related responsibilities. On the other side of the coin they fall easy prey to corruption and exploitation from petty government officials and would not raise their voice, for example, against the large-scale faulty installation of waterpipes in the villages - some of which do not function even on day one - or the faulty construction of village schools and roads, poor medical services, rampant corruption in revenue departments and block development offices. They need persuasion to adopt any innovation. They are quite content with their lifestyle and have no inclination to tune it to the needs of the day. A good example of this is the comparison of shops and roadside eating places in the villages and on main roads. The local owner of an establishment for decades would do little to improve the cleanliness and service, even though he would be earning a lot. As against the plainsman, who may have set up his business only a few years back but has prospered faster by applying imagination and better service. In contrast to the people who live in villages, those educated and even uneducated who take to outside employment and other vocations do extremely well by their intelligent and hard work. Obviously the need has driven people to find wealth and prosperity beyond the boundaries of their own districts. People from Uttarakhand have excelled mostly in employment in the armed forces, civil service, tourist trade, and as artists, journalists and mountaineers. But the region is still backward, poor and underdeveloped.

Languages spoken in Uttarakhand are Garhwali and Kumaoni in their respective divisions. There are, however, many dialects from district to district. People are bilingual: they can speak the Hindustani or Hindi of the plains. It is regrettable that present-generation children of Uttarakhand now settled in cities have taken to Hindi as their house language and cannot speak Garhwali or Kumaoni. This trend of speaking in Hindi has also developed in towns and on pilgrimage routes. Almost all educated people in the villages and shopkeepers can understand some English, if spoken slowly. Those with college education speak English, though with some hesitation.

EDUCATION

There were very few regular schools in Uttarakhand up to the nineteenth century. In those days, formal education was considered the exclusive privilege of Brahmins. Some of them were great scholars of Sanskrit, Ayurved and astrology, however there were hardly any schools teaching these subjects - the knowledge was mostly passed down the family line. It is believed that there were only about 121 Hindi and Sanskrit primary schools throughout Uttarakhand in 1850. The educational system was improved a bit during the British Raj, then serious efforts were made to popularise education after the independence of the country, as can be seen from the following table of schools opened.

	Before Independence Records Of 1942	24 Years After Independence Records Of 1971
Primary schools	1535	5197
Middle/senior schools	40	668
High schools	10	263
Intermediate colleges	8	25+
Degree colleges	2	15+

Recently many more schools and colleges have been opened and there are two separate universities and one agricultural university to cater for Garhwal and Kumaon divisions. Fees for schools and colleges run by the state are low so that most people can afford to send their children to school. There are scholarships and other incentives such as reserved places for bright students, certain casts and tribes, etc.

There are, however, peculiar conditions in the villages which require that children share the responsibility of farming and minding the livestock. As a result, many in far-flung areas are still reluctant to send their children to school as they need extra working hands at home. The ratio of educated males is higher than females. There is a very high level of unemployment.

In addition to state schools and colleges there are several private and public schools for wealthy people. Foreign missionaries introduced the English public school system in Uttarakhand during the British rule, and most were located in popular hill stations like Nainital, Mussoorie and Dehra Dun. Some of these schools are amongst the best in the country; the villagers, however, are not benefited by these schools.

The state has also introduced some specialised schools such as the Sainik military schools and Central schools for the children of central government employees on transferable jobs. These schools share the same educational syllabus. Sanskrit schools and job oriented vocational training schools have also been introduced. Most are co-educational but there are still a few schools and colleges exclusively for girls.

ROADS
During British rule the hill resorts of Mussoorie, Nainital, Ranikhet, Pauri and Lansdown were developed. However, the area was closed for two decades in 1958 at precisely the time the trekking industry boomed in Nepal and Kashmir. The area received no publicity and Uttarakhand became unknown Himalaya - a name few outside of mountaineering even know. During that time a remarkable road system was built through the valleys with the purpose of strengthening borders, improving transportation between important villages and promoting pilgrimage by transport to previously remote Hindu temples.

The main roads to centres of pilgrimage and strategically important destinations are built and maintained by an efficient paramilitary organisation, while other link roads are taken care of by the state's Public Works Department. During the rainy season road maintenance units are placed closer to all vulnerable sections to clear landslides and road blockages within a few hours of occurrence. It is rare for a road to remain blocked for more than a day or two, though in the case of a heavy landslide or road sinkage, a road can remain blocked for several days. When road blockages are expected to last several hours, transshipment of travellers is arranged using the vehicles stranded on the other side of the blockages. This works well as long as the vehicles have enough fuel supplies. Despite all efforts to maintain them, road conditions remain rather bad during the monsoon, calling for very careful driving on the bumpy, damaged roads. Accidents or vehicles veering off the road are rare - about three or four vehicles in a four-month season out of hundreds passing every day.

POLITICAL ADMINISTRATION

Until 1967 both Garhwal and Kumaon were administered through a commissioner with headquarters at Nainital. In 1968 two separate divisions were created to facilitate development. The districts of Pauri, Tehri, Dehra Dun, Chamoli and Uttarkashi became Garhwal division under a commissioner with headquarters at Pauri, and Kumaon division retained the districts of Nainital, Almora, Pithoragarh and Udhamsingh Nagar. In 1997 three more districts, Champawat, Bageshwar and Rudraprayag, were carved out to facilitate administration. Each district is headed by a District Magistrate. The districts are further split into subdivisions headed by a Subdivisional Magistrate, and each subdivision is further divided into tehsils and patties, headed by Tehsildar and Lekhpal respectively.

To settle minor disputes and to encourage participation in state developmental and welfare schemes, panchayat or village councils are formed. Each panchayat will have five to seven elected representatives and a Pradhan to head them. They sort out minor disputes and are supposed to protect the rights of the villagers and see how best they can be helped to improve their lot by way of development sought from the various sections of government: police, public works, education, medicine, electricity, irrigation, drinking water, agriculture, horticulture, fisheries, forestry and block development departments who function under the direct administrative control of the District Magistrate.

SOCIAL TRADITIONS AND CUSTOMS

The people tend to continue to practise their own traditions and customs. Houses are built after careful astrological consultation to ensure that the site is free from the influence of any evil spirit and there are no *Bhed*, or unlucky influences. Each village has its deity to protect them and their cattle. Houses are built below the village temple, and special prayers are offered at the end of every harvest and on certain other religiously important days. When anyone is in

25

distress of any kind, the Ghantwals, Bakya, or 'calculators', are consulted. The 'calculator' falls into a fit and in incoherent language declares the cause of the trouble and the deity who must be pleased. Sometimes a special ritual called *Jagar* is prescribed when men and women assemble at the house of the suffering family. *Jagri* is the man with a small drum who invokes by singing the spirit of the deity. Someone possessing the spirit starts dancing and prescribes certain actions to be taken by the suffering family to ward off the troubles. Having done as directed, sometimes the troubles are over but, when not, more sorcerers are consulted and many complicated actions are prescribed - years may be spent without achieving any results. One classic example is the belief that a women will not be able to bear a child or her children will not survive because of the influence of a ghost on her, perhaps because of her fall near a cremation ground.

Many of the fairs and festivals held throughout the year at various places are associated with a deity or to mark important occasions such as:

Haryala Festival Of Kumaon

This festival, celebrated to help ensure a good monsoon crop, takes place on the first solar day in the month of July. Five or seven different kinds of grain are sown by the lady of the house a few days before the festival, from a special basket, and watered. One day before the festival an image of the family deity is placed between the new shoots and prayers are offered on the day of the festival by the family priest.

Makar Sankranti

This is celebrated in January when the sun crosses over the Tropic of Cancer in a northerly direction. On this day a dip in the holy Ganges is considered a very auspicious start to the year. The festival is celebrated differently in different areas. It is called Magh Mela in Uttarkashi, where idols of gods and goddesses are brought from villages in great ceremony to the accompaniment of beating drums. Thousands of people from far and near assemble to participate in several cultural activities.

Vasant Panchmi

This is celebrated to welcome the spring, in February. Barley saplings specially sown for the occasion are collected and distributed among the families. People stick the saplings on both sides of their doors with cow dung, where it remains intact till the following year. The children wear something yellow.

Phool Sankranti

Phool (flower) Sankranti is celebrated in March when the spring flowers are in bloom. Children collect flowers in small baskets and go to sprinkle petals on the floor of each house in the village, wishing the people happiness. In return they get some money and special delicacies to eat.

Marriage

Marriage is usually arranged by parents after matching the horoscopes of the boy and girl. They must belong to the same level of cast (eg. Brahmin, Rajput) and have the approval of both families. Parents usually have the greater say in selecting a family for the relationship, though the system is gradually changing: now boys and girls may reject or approve each other, and may choose their spouse from within the cast, with parental approval. Intercast or love marriages are rare and usually regarded by parents as socially unacceptable. Sometimes children marrying against the wishes of parents are ousted from the family and social circle, and it can take them several months or even years to become reconciled with their family circle.

After finalising a match, an auspicious day is fixed by the family priest for engagement. Close family members, priest and friends of the boy's family visit the girl's house with ornaments or a ring, clothes for the girl, sweets and other gifts. Members of this party may number from 2-3 to thirty or forty or more depending on the status or consent of both families. Rings are exchanged between boy and girl at a ceremony conducted by the priest and presents in cash and kind are exchanged between the two families. It is customary for the girl's parents to include a number of utensils as gifts. A feast is organised for the guests of both families. On the day of engagement or soon after, the priest is approached to recommend a date for the marriage. The marriage ceremony itself is long and performed strictly under Vedic rites, involving several rituals. The groom's party may consist of just two or three or as many as four to five hundred, as mutually agreed by both parties, and are joined by the bride's guests at her house. The slow procession is accompanied by drums and other instruments, with some of the groom's guests dancing. On arrival at the bride's house a welcome ceremony is performed by priests, parents of the bride and their relations, followed by tea and lavish snacks. The bride's priest conducts a Tilak ceremony by applying a red mark called *Pithai* on the forehead of each of the groom's guests and presents an envelope containing money to each of them: it may be two or hundreds of rupees depending on the status of the girl's parents. After several rituals a big feast is served. The appointed time (*Lagna*) for the main marriage ceremony is when the bride and groom, joined by two pieces of yellow clothing around their waists, walk around the fire (made with selected wood such as peepul and mango) seven times while the priests chant holy scripts in Sanskrit, translating the meaning by actions where necessary. Two women sing Mangal (ceremonial songs) throughout the ceremony. It is usual for the bride's girlfriends to make fun of the groom and his party by passing all kinds of funny remarks, and the groom's party retaliates in kind!

At the end of the seventh round of the fire, certain obligations applicable to the bride and groom for a successful married life are spelled out by the priest for acceptance by both; for example, that they will remain faithful to each other, will jointly look after the children, will participate together in religious ceremonies, etc. Both nod their head in acceptance of these obligations and are then pronounced man and wife by the priest. The husband applies *Kumkum*, a red colour, on the bride's hair parting, which becomes part of her makeup as long as the husband is alive. After this they change seats; the wife from now on always sits on the left of the husband at all religious functions. The ceremony is completed next morning when Gaya Daan, a ritual in the presence of a cow, is performed. The cow's feet are washed by the girl's family and it is offered something to eat. Then the newly married couple with the bride's parents and close relatives walk around the cow, touching its feet, seeking blessing. At the end of the ceremony the cow is supposed to be presented to the groom, but with modern living conditions it is not possible for most to keep the cow, so a shortcut is to accept some money (not the market cost) in lieu.

After meals the time comes for the departure, or Tilak, ceremony and finally the departure of the groom and party along with the bride to his house. It is a very touching farewell. The bride, usually in tears, touches the feet of all the elders of her family. Her parents, sisters and close relations will also usually be in tears. It is the privilege of the brother to carry his bride sister some distance from the house to board her transport or to commence the journey to her in-laws' house with her husband.

Back at the groom's home, there are further ceremonies, rituals and feasts. It is completed with a thanksgiving ceremony called Satynarayan Katha at which the Almighty is remembered and thanked for His blessings.

It is the custom in most villages that the elder brother and younger brother's wife must not touch each other. If they touch by accident, a bath is prescribed for both. With the spread of education and people living in town, however, the custom is gradually fading away. When a member of the family or a close relative is leaving for another place, he or she is given something sweet to eat and a drop of yoghurt is applied on the forehead, or a pot filled with water is placed for good luck outside the door through which the person would be passing. Sneezing by anyone just before departure or before doing any work is considered a bad omen and the departure or work must be delayed by a few minutes. It is also considered unlucky for three people to set out from the same house together for work; if they have to, one will set off a bit early or late and join the other two further on. After a birth, the baby and mother are considered unclean for eleven days and are segregated, usually on the ground floor, where they must not be touched by anyone and the mother must take her own and the baby's clothes to the river for washing. In exceptional circumstances the period of segregation may be reduced to nine or seven days. At the end of it, a ceremony is performed before the idol of Ganesha (elephant god) by the priest and a name is given to the child.

A common form of greeting is to join palms, raising them in front of the face, and say *Namaskar* or *Namaste*. It will be responded to in the same manner. To greet an elder person in the family or the family priest, the feet of the person are touched with the palms joined together. The elder will say *Chiranjeev* or *Ayushman* (meaning 'have long life'). There is no equivalent form of greetings such as good morning, good night, etc, though *Dhanyabad* or *Meharbani* is said, with palms joined, to express gratitude. One should not sleep with feet pointing towards the head of the guest or an elder. A temple should be entered only after washing both feet and hands, or, by the more orthodox, after a bath. To be vegetarian or non-vegetarian is usually a personal preference and there is no stigma attached to either.

It is customary for guests to be asked repeatedly whether they would like to eat or drink, or to stay the night. If not, a guest would assume that the host was not genuine in his/her hospitality and would feel offended - even if the guest actually did not want to eat any more or had to leave on urgent business! A guest should reply politely that he/she has had enough and take just a tiny bit more to please the host, but try not to leave any food on the plate.

When a family member dies, no one in or closely related to the family will take any meals that night. The younger male members of the family usually shave their heads as an expression of mourning. Children, on death, are buried; others are cremated on the bank of a river. Women and children with parents alive do not attend the cremation. No marriages or festivities take place in the family of the deceased for one year, though in certain exceptional circumstances a marriage may be solemnised six months later. The eldest son or brother of the deceased has to perform certain rituals for twelve days: he sleeps on the floor of the room in which the death occurred, with a mustard oil lamp burning. He will eat only one meal a day, without salt, and is not permitted to shave. The twelfth day ritual conducted by the priest is called Dwadash or Terhwin. A meal is served to guests. Those who shaved their heads wear a new white cap. In addition, certain monthly rituals have to be performed for twelve months by the elder son or brother of the deceased. It is believed that the soul of the dead passes through several places over twelve months, then settles down as per the deeds of the previous life. The family dead are remembered on all religious occasions and every year during September/October when the eldest male performs a ritual called Shradh to pay homage to the dead.

RELIGION

The hills are the birthplace of the Hindu religion. But it is a historical reality that any religion or society does not survive forever on the value or necessity on which it was based. Intellectuals start criticizing the system and adopting new principles under the changed realities of life. Yardsticks of the religions and traditions also start changing. It was probably under such circumstances that Hinduism suffered a setback with the popularity of Budhism for some time. Early in the first century Budhism was at its prime in north India, including Uttarakhand. By about AD 700 some sort of change had taken place in Budhism and a great saint called Shankaracharya took upon himself to rejuvenate Hinduism. Vedas and Purans began to receive importance once again. Shankaracharya got the temples in north India repaired, constructed the Vishnu temple in Badrinath and established a centre for learning at Joshimath. Saint Shankaracharya was born in Malabar, south India. By the time he was twelve, he had received enlightenment in all the Vedas and Puranas. At the age of eleven he came to Badrinath to live and meditate. He died at the age of thirty-two. The temples of Yamnotri, Gangotri, Kedarnath, the Panchkedar and Panchbadri were established long ago along with Badrinath.

Most of the Hindu saints and sages of ancient India such as Vyas, Vashishtha, Budha and Shankaracharya have spent time meditating in Uttarakhand to gain self-confidence and willpower. The region was therefore called Tapobhumi (land of meditation). According to the Hindu scripture the great gods and goddesses walked and conversed with sages and ascetics in Uttarakhand. Here the deeds of the Pandava brothers of the epic *Mahabharata* are recalled in song and dance by the hillfolk. The Pandavas are believed to have finished their earthly pilgrimage here, seeking heaven. Hanuman, the monkey god, also underwent stern austerities in Langurgarh. To this day thousands of Hindus seek salvation by pilgrimage to the holy temples. Maharshsi Vedbyas described the religious importance of the places of this region in the Hindu scripture *Skandhapurana* thousands of years ago. There have since been changes in the names of the places mentioned in the *Skandhapurana*, which can only be guessed from their description now; for example, Tamsa river is now called Tons, and Gangadwar is now Hardwar.

PART II
Tourism

Uttarakhand has not only been drawing Hindu pilgrims from all over the world, but also the charm of its Himalayan peaks have been attracting foreign explorers and mountaineers for over a hundred years. The well-known peaks of Nandadevi, Kamet, Trishul, Changbhang, Dunagiri, Mana, Chaukhamba, Nandakot, Shivling, Mrigthuni, Bhagirathi, Banderpunch, Kalanka, Bethartoli, Hardeol, Panchchuli, Nandaghunti etc. are located here. The hill scenery is rugged and rarely terraced outside the main valleys. The trekking routes pass through villages, forests and open meadows. The forests hold a great deal of wildlife, birds and butterflies. There is something of interest for everyone in Uttarakhand in terms of human interest, natural beauty, fascinating legends and unsurpassed mountain panoramas.

Trekking and tourism to all Himalayan areas continues to increase dramatically. With Laddakh and Nepal overflowing, tourists and the travel industry are looking elsewhere in the Himalaya for new destinations. The obvious choice is Uttarakhand and although by comparison with other Himalayan areas it is little visited at present, that situation is changing rapidly. The exploits and books of Tilman, Shipton and Smyth popularised the area before World War II. During British rule some hill stations were developed. Everything seems set for a boom in trekking and adventure tourism in Uttarakhand. It offers easy access and a unique cultural and scenic experience.

With the growth of facilities and the multifarious, busy life of today, tourism has ceased to be the leisurely, homely cottage industry it used to be. It has burst upon the world as a modern, sophisticated, major industry. It now calls for a massive investment in capital, enterprise know-how, infrastructure, human understanding, eating and living facilities, travel information and organisations to handle fast tourist movements. Though the travel trade and the government have realised the potential of this region

Baijnath Temple (Photo: Anup Shah)
The Himalaya from Mussoorie (Photo: Anup Shah)

Kumaon girls in traditional dress (Photo: Anup Shah)
Badrinath (Photo: Author)

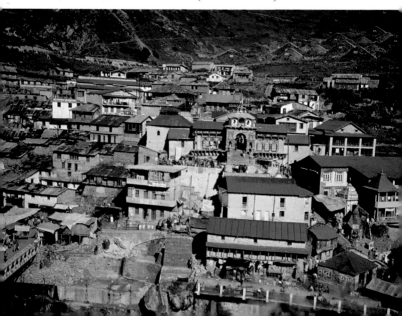

and are trying to develop some infrastructure, a lot more is needed to be done. A traveller to Uttarakhand must therefore be mentally prepared to rough it a little, especially if travelling independently, and be careful in selecting the tour operator, clarifying in advance the services required, and yet be prepared to take life as it comes. One should not compare or expect the efficiency of developed countries here. To enjoy a kick out of life one must learn to experience the contrasts of life. A visitor must not be surprised that the government tourist agencies lack professionalism. If you approach a government agency for information or assistance, be prepared for delays or a vague bureaucratic reply! It is safe for an individual to tour Uttarakhand economically without going through a tour operator, but one needs to have patience during delays and be prepared to eat local food.

UP Tourism has offices in some state capitals of the country and important hill stations. The Kumaon Mandal Vikas Nigam (KMVN) and Garhwal Mandal Vikas Nigam (GMVN) are the tourism-promoting state government agencies within Kumaon and Garhwal. Apart from offering package tours to cater basically for Indians, they also manage tourist bungalows and travellers' lodges within their regions (see Accommodation). There are private tour operators, some of which provide all-inclusive, excellent services and are prompt in responding to queries.

You should go to Uttarakhand with an open mind, to enjoy its heritage and to see a mini India through its temples. The religious sentiments and social customs of the people must be respected. Entry to some parts of Uttarakhand is either restricted or banned: you cannot go there without entry permits granted by central government. Photography is permitted but photographing bridges, military installations and the inside of temples is strictly prohibited. Shooting of birds and wildlife is prohibited. Flowers, seeds and bulbs are not permitted to be taken out of national parks. In the case of serious ailments or accidents requiring evacuation from the mountains, helicopter rescue can be requested through the District Magistrate, who can be contacted through any police post, wireless station or any government official available nearby with means to contact the authorities. All civil hospitals accept out-patients for consultations and treatment free of charge provided the medicines are available in the hospital. In emergencies, even military and paramilitary medical posts will help.

For travel to Kumaon the railheads are Kathgodam and Tanakapur connected to Delhi and Lucknow by overnight trains. Bus connections or taxis are available from railheads for Nainital, Almora, Ranikhet, Pithoragarh and any other place. Public transport fares are fixed by the government and usually displayed at the ticket counter. Departure times must be checked at the bus station. The punctuality of public bus services is unreliable; travellers must be prepared for delays. Taxis and chartered bus services are operated by local operators and are easy to locate near the railway station and bus stand. Rates must, however, be negotiated in advance and details of services clarified with them.

The nearest airport for Kumaon is Pantnagar, connected by a flight serving Delhi and Lucknow. The frequency of flights is not reliable at present. Advance booking of seats is possible for air, train and certain deluxe public buses and any transport provided by tour operators. Direct bus services are also available from Inter State Bus Terminus (ISBT) Delhi to several towns in Kumaon and Garhwal.

Hardwar, Rishikesh, Dehra Dun and Kotdwar are the railheads to Garhwal. All these places are connected by several trains with Delhi, Calcutta, Bombay and Lucknow. Dehra Dun airport at Jollygrant serving Mussoorie and Hardwar is connected by a 40-minute flight from Delhi which is currently not operating. There is also a fast day train, the Shatabdi Express, from New Delhi to Hardwar, Dehra Dun and back. A convenient overnight train from Delhi to Dehra Dun is the Mussoorie Express, which also stops at Hardwar next morning at 0600 for a connection to Rishikesh. The Mussoorie Express leaves Old Delhi at 2220, arriving at Dehra Dun next morning at 0800. Return of the train from Dehra Dun is at 2100, arriving at Delhi next morning at 0700. Air-conditioned, first and second class sleeping berths can be reserved a month in advance.

ACCOMMODATION
In cities like Dehra Dun, Rishikesh, Mussoorie, Nainital, Almora and Ranikhet, hotels of all categories are available. In pilgrimage centres Dharamshalas (charitable rest houses) and Ashrams have been established by industrialists and religious organisations. You

can stay in Dharamshalas and Ashrams by paying a small amount for sharing dormitory accommodation. Here the communal toilets and private facilities are rather dirty; some also provide bedding which is often unclean. With the rush of pilgrims, they just cannot cope with all the cleaning and washing, so you are advised to carry a sleeping bag while travelling in Uttarakhand. Some Indians have a habit of chewing Paan (betel) stuffed with various ingredients, including tobacco, which makes the mouth red. They spit it out anywhere, including bedroom walls, stair cases, toilet corners etc. One European woman once complained to me that someone had perhaps used the corner of her room as a toilet in an emergency and had not cleaned it up! Greatly alarmed, when I went to her room it was the spit of the dreadful Paan. In a nutshell, a comfort-loving European would describe the accommodation intended for middle-income group pilgrims as 'awful to basic'. Some of the Dharamshalas and Ashrams have a few rooms with two to three beds each, with cleaner bedding and private facilities; such rooms cost a bit more but are in great demand. These places include the tourist bungalows and travellers' lodges, but they tend to be very noisy and disorganised with a large number of groups checking in and out. On pilgrimage routes it is very common to find pilgrims singing devotional songs loudly, at any time of the day and night, unmindful of the next-door neighbour sleeping or being ill. Usually devotees get up around 4am to prepare for going to temples, making a lot of noise. The hot water and tea sellers start banging the doors in their effort to sell *Garampani* and *Chaa* (hot water and tea). It is to some extent unavoidable when a large cross-section of people are using the limited facilities. The accommodation in pilgrim centres is expected to cater for as many people as possible. It is not uncommon to find four or eight people sharing a double bedroom or twenty people sleeping on the floor of a room meant for ten during peak season. With a short pilgrimage / tourist season, running expensive hotels is not viable.

Reservations for KMVN and GMVN accommodation are confirmed on advance payment. It is best to approach the Reservations Office or unit concerned on arrival - you may never get a response to your letters from these agencies, as experienced by Indian tour operators! The author is a regular victim of unacknowledged letters and unhonoured commitments. Once, breakfast ordered at 8am in a tourist bungalow at the Auli ski resort was not served till 10am and the manager was not available to hear the complaint because he was "still sleeping and was not to be disturbed". This is not an isolated example. The geysers or toilets may not be functioning. In certain bungalows without electricity, even candles are not provided. Accommodation rates vary considerably and keep changing every year.

Despite these difficulties, the tourist bungalows and travellers' lodges managed by the KMVN and GMVN have on the whole better accommodation than the Dharamshalas and Ashrams. Below are details of their facilities. Number of beds given against each represent the total for both double rooms and dormitories. All rooms are non-air-conditioned.

KMVN - Managed Accommodation

NAINITAL REGION

Nainital	Tourist reception centre, Sukhatal Mallital	136 beds
	Tourist reception centres, Tallital	120 beds
Bhimtal	Tourist bungalow	50 beds
Sattal	" "	10 beds
Bhowali	" "	30 beds
Kathgodam	" "	16 beds
Ramnagar	" "	57 beds

(30km from Corbet National Park)

ALMORA REGION

Almora	Holiday home	76 beds
Kausani	Tourist bungalow	104 beds
Ranikhet	" "	52 beds
Sitlakhet	" "	20 beds
Jageshwar	" "	30 beds
Bageshwar	" "	60 beds
Binsar	" "	40 beds

Pindari Glacier Trekking Route

Loharkhet	" "	12 beds
Dhakuri	" "	12 beds
Khati	" "	12 beds
Dwali	" "	12 beds
Phurkia	" "	12 beds

PITHORAGARH REGION

Pithragarh	"	"	24 beds
Champawat	"	"	20 beds
Lohaghat	"	"	20 beds
Chaukori	"	"	16 beds

GMVM - Managed Accommodation

GARHWAL REGION

Source of Ganges Trekking Route

Dehra Dun	160 beds	Mussoorie	75 beds
Dhanolti	20 beds	Chamba	20 beds
Uttarkashi	112 beds	Bhaironghati	30 beds
Gangotri	88 beds	Bhojbasa	38 beds

Yamnotri Route

Barkot	36 beds	Sayanchatti	18 beds
Hanumanchatti	30 beds	Jankichatti	76 beds

Har-ki-doon Trekking Route

Dakpather	36 beds	Taluka	10 beds
Osla	10 beds		

Rishikesh-Kedarnath Route

Rishikesh (Muni ki Reti)	102 beds	Devprayag	40 beds
Srinagar	204 beds	Guptkashi	44 beds
Sonprayag	47 beds	Gauri Kund	40 beds
Kedarnath	33 beds		

Rishikesh-Badrinath Route

Rudraprayag	127 beds	Gauchar	28 beds
Karanprayag	38 beds	Nandprayag	30 beds
Pipalkoti	38 beds	Joshimath	74 beds
Auli	116 beds	Ghangharia	72 beds
Badrinath	84 beds		

Rishikesh-Karanprayag-Rupkund Trekking Route

Gwaldom	20 beds	Deval	14 beds
Mundoli (Lohjung)	15 beds	Wan	12 beds

Rishikesh-Pauri Route

Chila	20 beds	Kotdwar	14 beds
Lansdowne	20 beds	Pauri	35 beds

Gopeshwar-Chopta Route

Gopeshwar	24 beds	Chopta	47 beds
Ukhimath	12 beds		

Some government departments such as forestry, public works and irrigation have set up their own rest houses with two or more rooms and private facilities for use by their travelling officials. If vacant, tourists are allowed to hire this accommodation, though the procedure for this is rather complicated. Sometimes you may have to travel several miles to find the right official to issue the bungalow permit, and the allotment already made to a tourist may be cancelled without notice if a government official turns up for the night. Caretakers called Chaukidars in some bungalows allow tourists to stay even without permits on condition that it will be vacated if the permit holder turns up. These bungalows do not provide catering services.

Schools
The school system in the villages is extensive, and if you ask for accommodation you may be taken to a schoolteacher who speaks a bit of English, and will often invite you to sleep in the school building. If you can communicate with each other well enough this is an ideal chance to learn something of village life, and in return to explain how you live at home. You will, of course, get many other curious visitors, and if you stay for the start of school you will hear the children singing prayers or the National Anthem first thing in the morning.

Private Houses
It is not a very regular occurrence to be invited into a private house, but individual trekkers or couples may be asked, perhaps by a respected community member who can speak a word or two of English, to accommodate you, though your room may sometimes be a verandah. It is not that the villagers are unfriendly, simply that resources of all kinds are scarce. Homes are usually more than full and the people have no room for you and are somewhat self-conscious. If you are invited in you will usually be offered a meal, which is cooked soon after dusk, and will find your hosts very attentive and courteous. Most homes contain extended families. The people rise early, starting the day with only tea and little breakfast and going to sleep after the evening meal. Remember spoons and forks are not used in villages. You should take care to

use your right hand to eat, and to be careful not to put your shoes on any bedding. Try and communicate your appreciation to your hosts, and if you have something suitable you could make a small gift.

Food

Roadside eating places provide simple Indian meals. A standard meal of Dal-Bhat (lentils with rice) with one vegetable today would cost as little as 35 cents at a cheap place. Foreigners or those with delicate stomachs must never drink unboiled water while passing through villages, towns and at eating places. Drinking water must be boiled. Alternatively drink tea, bottled soft drinks or mineral water.

During monsoons when roads are blocked due to landslides, traffic may be held up at places and there may be an acute shortage of food supplies till the road is cleared. A traveller is advised always to carry some reserve food to meet any such emergencies. By and large essential, basic provisions can be purchased anywhere in shops on the pilgrim routes, roads and village shops except when there is no flow of supplies from the plains for any reason. It is worth noting that a landslide may occur where there are no shops near the road blockage, or maybe so many vehicles are stranded that the roadside shops run out of provisions. As it is, supplies to the hills are irregular.

MAIN TOWNS AND HILL STATIONS

The British developed Mussoorie, Nainital, Ranikhet, Almora and Lansdowne as hill resorts to escape the heat of the plains. Since independence, many resorts have been developed as tourist attractions. Some of the main resorts and towns are as follows.

Dehra Dun

Surrounded on the east by the Ganga and on the west by the Yamuna, the Doon Valley is most picturesque at the foothills of the Shivalik ranges. Dehra Dun is one of the most beautiful towns of northern India. It has a number of educational institutions of repute including the Indian Military Academy, Forest Research Institute, Training Centre for the Blind, Wadia Institute of Himalayan Studies,

Headquarters of the Surveyor General of India, and the Oil and Natural Gas Commission. It is connected by regular public transport to several towns of northern India and major pilgrimage centres in Garhwal. There are very good hotels, tours and travel agencies, medical and utility services. It is a take-off point to some very interesting tourist and trekking destinations which are covered elsewhere in the book. According to legend, in the period of Mahabaharata, Guru Dronacharya was in search of a peaceful and lovely place where he could meditate and he came to Dehra Dun. Hence the whole valley of Doon was called Drona Ashram, 'the abode of Drona', which is probably the derivation of the present name Dehra Dun.

Approach: Connected to New Delhi and all the important cities of India by comfortable trains. Public buses and taxis also ply between Dehra Dun and many cities, towns and all the district headquarters of Uttarakhand districts. It is 255km by road from Delhi, 54km from Hardwar and 42km from Rishikesh.

Accommodation: There are one- to four-star category hotels. Accommodation is readily available. Rates vary considerably according to facilities, and taxes are additional.

Places Of Interest: The sulphur springs of Sahastradhara 14km, Forest Research Institute and its five very educative museums 5km, and Malsi Deer Park 9km. The Paltan Bazar is a very interesting market-place and less expensive than Delhi or Agra for tourists.

Hardwar
Literally 'the doorway to God', Hardwar is by far the most popular centre of Hinduism, situated on the banks of the Ganga at the foot of the Shivalik hills. It is visited by millions of Hindu devotees every year to take a dip in the sacred Ganga for emancipation from sins. It is one of the four pilgrim centres of the religious festival Kumbh, held every twelve years, for which elaborate preparations are made over a year in advance to receive millions of tourists. The next Kumbh Festival will be held in the year 2010. There are many temples and abodes of saints, called Ashrams, visited by the pilgrims. It is an extraordinary experience to see hundreds of devotees at any time of the day performing religious rituals or taking a holy dip in

the Ganga at Har-ki-Pauri. One must not miss the evening prayers at the Har-ki-Pauri when hundreds of oil lamps are floated on the river. Close by is the Mansa Devi Temple, reached by a ropeway. Besides providing a panoramic view of the valley below, offering prayers at this temple, and tying a thread on a banyan tree with a wish, is believed to fulfil it. A visit to the temple has to be repeated when the wish is granted. Among the most important temples are Ganga and Shankaracharya near Har-ki-Pauri and Chandi Devi, 3km away.

Approach: It is reached from New Delhi and all main cities of India by comfortable trains, public transport and taxis. Hardwar is en route to Dehra Dun by train. It also provides a connection to Rishikesh, 24km, and to the shrines of Badrinath, Kedarnath, Yamunotri and Gangotri by taxi and public transport. There are many tour operators to assist travellers. Hire charges of taxis are prominently displayed at the taxi stand just outside the railway station.

Accommodation: There are several Dharamshalas (charitable rest houses) and hotels catering for vegetarians. Alcoholic drinks and non-vegetarian meals are not permitted because of its religious sanctity.

Rishikesh
A celebrated spiritual centre, Rishikesh has been the venue of many international personalities including The Beatles. This holy city, 45 minutes' drive from Hardwar, is situated on the right bank of the Ganga. Laxman, brother of Lord Rama, incarnation of Vishnu, is believed to have selected this place for hard penance in order to get rid of the sin of slaying Brahmins in the Ram-Rawan battle. Saints and sages lived in caves and meditated here in ancient days. Comfortable Ashrams have now been set up by learned saints. Prominent among such Ashrams are Shivanand Ashram (run by the Divine Life Society), Kailash Ashram and Parmarth Niketan. It is the gateway to all four Himalayan shrines and to most of the trekking destinations. Tour operators are available. On the left bank of the Ganga are Gita Bhawan, Swargashram, and Maharishi Mahesh Yogi's Meditation Centre which has 84 cavernous rooms with all modern facilities. Apart from organising meditation and Hindu

41

religious discourses, some of these Ashrams, such as Shivanand Ashram, organise yoga training. Devotees come to spend a few days in these Ashrams to meditate and listen to the religious discourses of learned saints. Rishikesh is a very interesting place to those who may want to know about Hinduism. Other places of interest in Rishikesh are the Ghats (bathing places in the Ganga), Bharat Mandir (Temple), Lakshman Temple about 6km away, Raghunath Temple and Pushkar Temple. The left bank can be reached by Laxman jhula and other bridges across the Ganga. There is also a boat service available from Munikireti to Swargashram. Many orange robe-clad Sadhus live here or stop over for a few days. There are several charitable kitchens where free food is served to Sadhus and beggars twice a day. These free kitchens are run by temple authorities, businesses and charitable trusts. Devotees contribute liberally towards this good cause. There is also a Gurudwara, place of worship of the Sikh, at Rishikesh where any person, irrespective of religious faith, is provided accommodation and free meals in the community kitchen. You are expected to observe the prescribed norms at a place of worship; for example, your head must be covered with a cap or cloth and you must not smoke in a Gurudwara.

Approach: Same as for Hardwar.

Accommodation: There are several Dharamshalas and hotels in different price ranges. The best hotels at present are Natraj Mandakini and Ganga kinare. Here also only vegetarian meals are provided and alcoholic drinks are not permitted.

Lansdowne
Named after the then British viceroy Lord Lansdowne, this was built by the British, at 1780m altitude, as a cantonment to train the famous Garhwali soldiers. Surrounded by thick oak forest, with great mountain views, it is a good place for a quiet holiday as there is not the usual hustle-bustle of the better known hill stations. It is 45km from the railhead at Kotdwar, served by overnight train from Delhi and Lucknow etc, and five hours' drive from Dehra Dun and four hours from Hardwar. Taxis and public transport are available. There is a tourist bungalow for accommodation. Its original name

is Kalon Danda (black forest) because of the mist created during the monsoon.

Pauri

At 1840m/5800ft altitude, Pauri is the headquarters of Garhwal division. It provides a 150km panorama of Mt. Bandar-Punch, Swargrohini, Gangotri, Kedarnath, Badrinath and Mt. Nanda Devi ranges. You can enjoy quiet walks in the direction of Bubakhal and Kandolia. Khirsu, 19km, at 1700m is another beautiful spot providing a closer panoramic view of the Garhwal Himalaya. You get the feeling of complete peace in the oak and deodar forest and apple orchards around Khirsu.

Approach: Kotdwar and Rishikesh are the nearest rail termini, both five hours' drive away. On completion of the new bridge over the Ganga at Devprayag the driving distance from Rishikesh will be reduced by an hour. Public transport and taxis are available at all places.

Accommodation: There is a tourist bungalow and some simple private hotels.

Joshimath

Winter place of the Rawal and other officials of Badrinath Temple, Joshimath is situated in the district of Chamoli at 1890m/6200ft and 45km from Badrinath. This beautifully situated town is sheltered by a circular ridge to the north. The Shankaracharya attained enlightenment here in a cave. Above the cave is the Kalpa Briksha (Mulbury tree) believed to be over 2000 years old. Joshimath is an important town link to the Niti and Mana valleys, beyond which is Tibet. Among the main temples there are Narsingh, Durga, Ganesh, Surya and the Nandadevi. The deity Narsingh, incarnation of Vishnu, is very important. The Rawal offers prayers at this temple during winter when Badrinath is closed. Joshimath is rapidly developing as an important town and tourist centre. It is gateway to Badrinath, Nandadevi sanctuary, Niti and Mana passes leading to Tibet, Kwari Pass, Valley of Flowers, and the ski slopes of Auli and Gorson. No-one is allowed to enter Nandadevi sanctuary or the Niti and Mana valleys without special permits granted by the District Magistrate, Chamoli.

Joshimath is connected to Auli ski resort, 13km, by road and by ropeway. Auli provides a grand panoramic view of Mt. Nandadevi, Hathi, Ghori, Nilkanth and Mana peaks.

Approach: The shortest approach route is from Rishikesh, 255km. Public transport or private coach/taxis are available on the main route.

Accommodation: There are two tourist bungalows and several hotels. Dronagiri, Nilkanth and Kamet are the best ones.

Mussoorie
Mussoorie is a fascinating hill resort at 2006m/6200ft and 35km from Dehra Dun. Its green hills and varied fauna and flora make it a colourful and picturesque hill station commanding a wonderful view of the extensive Banderpunch-Gangotri ranges of Himalaya to the north-west. Its history dates back to 1827 when Captain Young, an adventurous British officer, discovered the present site, which was used as a holiday resort for British troops. There are the usual travel facilities. Mussoorie has some highly reputable educational institutions where children from all over the world come as boarders. It is conveniently connected by road to Delhi via Dehra Dun and is also the gateway to Yamnotri and Gangotri shrines. Short excursions and places to see around Mussoorie are:

Kempty Falls: 12km along the Yamnotri road is the biggest and prettiest waterfall, located in a beautiful valley.

Municipal Gardens: A picnic spot 4km away with a beautiful garden and a small artificial lake.

Camel's Back Road: This 3km road starts from Kulri Bazar near Rink hall and ends at Library Bazar. It is a very enjoyable walk through attractive shops and provides a superb sunset view.

Gun Hill: Offers a beautiful panoramic view of the Garhwal Himalaya extending from Banderpunch to Gangotri ranges. A 400m ropeway connects Gun Hill with Mall Road near the tourist office. During the British Raj a gun mounted on this top used to be fired to herald midday so people could adjust their watches - hence this name.

Dhanolti: Located on the Mussoorie-Tehri-Gangotri road at 25km it offers a captivating view of over 300km of the Garhwal Himalaya.

It is situated at about 2400m in the midst of pine and deodar forest and is ideal for quiet holidays. There is a reasonably good hotel and a tourist bungalow with restaurant facilities. From here you can drive 7km up to Kadukhal and make a 1.5km trek to the Surkanda Devi Temple at 3200m, which offers a grand panoramic view of the Himalaya.

Accommodation: There are several hotels, some of them five-star. Most of the hotels offer heavily reduced rates during the winter and the monsoon period.

Chakrata

(At present entry to the entire subdivision of Chakrata is closed to foreigners.)

Situated at 2135m/6960ft altitude and a 92km drive from Dehra Dun, Chakrata is known for its serene environment and sylvan charm. The northern part of Chakrata is covered with dense forest and dotted with villages and provides a fascinating 2-3 day trek. Deoband at 2860m/9400ft and Mundali (almost the same height) provide great panoramic views of the Garhwal Himalaya. This will turn out to be the most popular all-season short and easy trekking destination for foreigners when at least a part of it opens, hopefully before 2000.

Almora

Almora is the district headquarters at 1646m/5450ft altitude. It is perched on a 5km-long saddle-shaped ridge with green terraced fields, sun-dappled pine forest and the ever present mountain panorama of the Pindari glacier region. It is famous for making traditional copper vessels in exquisite shapes.

Approach: Kathgodam is the nearest railway station, 92km, linked by overnight trains from Delhi and Lucknow. Regular buses and private taxis ply to Almora from these places.

Accommodation: There are several Indian-style hotels including a tourist bungalow.

Places Of Interest: Apart from an interesting market, famous for copper vessels, and sweets called Bal Mithai, there are pleasant walks to places like Bright end corner, just 2km along the main road which provides a lovely view of snow-covered peaks at sunset and sunrise. Simtola, 4km, and Kalimati, 1km, are well known for pine forests, flower nurseries and orchards. Excursion tours are available to the following places:

Katramal: 16km. Famous for the 12th century sun temple. The brown stone idol of the sun is 1.1m high and 60cm wide.

Jageshwar: 34km drive on the way to Pithoragarh through a very beautiful narrow valley hedged by tall ancient deodar trees. It is famous for fine sculptured Hindu temples with profuse floral carvings of over 100 small and large shrines. It is connected by regular bus services with Nainital and Almora. There is a tourist bungalow.

Baijnath: 71km, 1125m/3750ft. A picturesque temple town on the banks of Baijnath river. A beautiful idol of the goddess Parvati is enshrined in the main temple. It also has many beautiful relics of 12th and 13th century sculptured stone including Ganesh, Chandrika, Kuber and Sungod. There is a museum maintained by the archaeological department.

Kausani: 53km, 1890m/6200ft. Famous for a grand view of the Garhwal and Kumaon Himalaya extending to over 200km. The Trishul-Nandadevi ranges are particularly spectacular and look incredibly close. This place has been the favourite of poets, philosophers and nature lovers. There is an Ashram run by Sarla Ben, an Indian-turned-American follower of Mahatma Gandhi.

Those travelling from Gwaldom to Almora/Nainital or vice versa will also pass through Kausani. It is well connected by public transport and has a tourist bungalow and a few hotels.

Binsar: 30km, 2241m/7100ft. A quiet retreat under oak and rhododendron trees. It offers a panoramic view of the countryside as well as a 200km stretch of Himalaya including Mt. Kedarnath, Chaukhamba, Trishul, Nandadevi, Nandakot and Panchachuli. The region abounds in alpine flora, ferns and lichen. There is no regular public bus service but taxis can be chartered through local tour operators from Nainital and Almora.

Chaukori: 2010m/6540ft, 112km from Pithoragarh, 75km from Almora and 145km from Nainital, connected by public bus transport and private taxis. It provides fabulously wide views of

16 peaks including Mt. Trishul, Nandadevi and Panchachuli ranges. It is a lovely place with oak, rhododendron and pine forest. There is a 16 bed tourist bungalow and some tent cottages. The mountains look spectacular at sunrise and sunset.

Excursion To Patal Bhubneshwari: 40km from Chaukori on the road to Berinag is the cave temple Patal Bhubneshwari, a geological marvel, 10m deep and 130m wide, in which many myths of Hinduism are immortalised by stone formations in various shapes, identifiable as Shesh-Nag (Cobra), Ganesh (Elephant god), Badrinath, Kedarnath, etc.

Another interesting excursion can be made to the musk deer breeding farm about 5km from Chaukori.

Nainital

A gem in perfect setting, this charming lake resort at 1938m/6300ft is also the district headquarters. A story goes that the Nayana (eye) of Lord Shiva's consort fell here, giving the lake the name Nayanatal, which led to its present name. Overlooking the lake is Nayana Devi temple, built in homage to the goddess. Graceful willows encircle the emerald mountain lake which is a little over 3km in circumference. During the day, the city is gay with brightly coloured tiny villas and bungalows. As the sun sets behind the mountains, the hill station turns into an enchanting, alluring fairyland, and rowing boats filled with happy holidaymakers sail on the shimmering waters. Ponies, rickshaws (hand-pulled carts) and people throng the lake promenade, which is lined with bazaars, restaurants and hotels. There are also some of the finest public schools in Nainital.

Approach Route: Nearest railhead is Kathgodam, 35km. It is also very well connected by public bus with Delhi and the main cities of north-west Uttar Pradesh. Local tour operators offer conducted sightseeing and trekking tours from Nainital.

Accommodation: There are several hotels of both Indian and western style. Most of them have different rates for different seasons. The high season is May to mid-July and the autumn season mid-September to the end of October. The remaining weeks are 'off season' when the rates are lowest. In low season, services such as hot water and room heaters need to be negotiated before hiring a room in any hotel. This advice holds good for all hill stations.

Places Of Interest:

Snow View: 2km away at 2270m/7200ft is a nice picnic spot. There is a powerful telescope fixed here to see the Himalayan panorama.

Naina Peak: Also called Cheena Peak, it is situated at 2611m/8250ft, about 6km of lovely walking, providing a panoramic view of the Himalaya in the distance and the valley below.

Hanuman Garh: 3km away (1951m/6150ft), with a lovely sunset view. There is also a famous temple of Hanuman, the monkey god. One kilometre beyond is the state astronomical observatory.

Sightseeing Tours:

Bhowali: 11km on the road to Ranikhet is a health resort at 1706m/5350ft in the middle of pine forest. It is also a famous fruit market for apples, apricots, peaches and plums. About 3km from here along a beautiful road is Ghorakhal, a charming quiet place with a public school for Indians.

Bhimtal: This second lake resort is 22km away (1371m/4300ft). The lake is larger than at Nainital and is a delightful place for boating and picnics. It is also good for birdwatching. There are simple but comfortable hotels.

Naukuchiatal: 1219m/3870ft. A pretty lake with nine corners (Naukuchi) which gives it its name. It is an excellent place for fishing and a haven for migratory birds. There is a tourist bungalow.

Sattal: 1828m/5750ft. A captivating and picturesque spot with seven interconnected lakes in the middle of pine and oak forest. Swimming and boating is possible here.

Ramgarh: 1789m/5630ft. Famous for orchards, bee-keeping and a commanding view of the Himalaya, Ramgarh is 26km along the Bhowali-Mukteshwar road.

Mukteshwar: 2286m/7250ft, 51km from Nainital. Besides being a celebrated spot of scenic beauty it is also the seat of the Indian Veterinary Research Institute. There are many apple orchards in this region.

Jeolkot: 1219m/3870ft, situated on the way up from Kathgodam, 18km short of Nainital. It is a health resort, popular for butterflies and bee-keeping.

Corbett National Park: 115km. Details of this park are given separately.

Pithoragarh

Pithoragarh is the district headquarters. The district borders Tibet in the north and Nepal in the east. Due to this strategic location, the outer limits due north and east are marked by an inner line beyond which no outsiders are permitted to go without a permit from India's Ministry of Home Affairs. The town is located in a picturesque and extensive valley and has many temples and remnants of historic fortifications dating back to the 16th century.

Approach: The nearest rail terminals are Kathgodam, 207km, and Tanakpur, 151km. It is linked with Nainital and Almora by public transport. Excursions and sightseeing tours are available from local tour operators from Nainital and Almora.

Accommodation: There are government rest houses, a tourist bungalow and simple hotels.

Places Of Interest And Excursions: Rai-Gufa (cave), very close to the town, carved out of limestone deposits. Another interesting place in the town is the Ulkadevi temple, an aspect of SHAKTI (power), situated on the hill top.

Champawat: 1615m / 5220ft, 75km on the way up to Pithoragarh from the railhead at Tanakpur and situated in a wide lush valley. It has the Baleshwar temple complex with its richly carved rock structures. There is a 'Ras Mandappam' with erotic carvings at the base. The sculpted symbols of 'Kirtimukh', row of diamonds and lotus on the pillars are reminiscent of medieval western Indian sculpture. The structure of Baleshwar temple is remarkable for its intricate carving. Accommodation is available.

Didihat: 54km north of Pithoragarh, connected by public transport, it commands an unsurpassable view of the Panchchuli group of peaks. There is very ordinary accommodation available.

Ranikhet

Ranikhet, 'Queens Field', 1830m / 5800ft, is idyllic in its charm, for holidaymakers almost all the year round. With its encircling snow-capped Himalayan peaks glistening in the sun, the town casts an instant spell on visitors. Ranikhet commands a view of the central

Himalaya. It was discovered and developed by the British in 1868, as a cantonment and hill resort to escape from the summer heat of the plains. It continues as a training centre for the Kumaon Regiments. It also has a golf course. There is a drug factory and herborium for research and production of Aurvedic medicines made from Himalayan herbs.

Approach: Nearest railhead is Kathgodam, 84km. It is well connected by public transport with Kathgodam, Almora (50km), Nainital (59km), Pithoragarh (169km), Bareilly (190km), Delhi (361km), and Gopeshwar via Karanprayag (145km).

Accommodation: There are western and Indian style hotels including some nice tourist cottages.

Places Of Interest:

Chaubatia: 10km from Ranikhet, with a state research station for fruit cultivation and several orchards.

MOUNTAINEERING, SKIING, FISHING, RIVER RUNNING
Mountaineering
The Garhwal Himalaya has been in the forefront for climbers since early this century, for Europeans and the British in particular. It received a great setback when in 1959 the entire region was closed for mountaineering to foreigners for about two decades. It was during that period that the mountains in Nepal attracted the attention of mountaineers and trekkers from all over the world, and the liberal policy of the Government of Nepal actively encouraged and popularised trekking and mountaineering here, and people almost forgot the Garhwal Himalaya. The Government of India began lifting the restriction on climbing from 1975 onwards, which made it possible for foreigners to climb again in the Garhwal and Kumaon Himalaya under certain conditions. There is still a considerable part of the Garhwal and Kumaon Himalaya which falls beyond the 'inner line' for security reasons, where foreigners and even non-local Indians are not allowed to enter without special permission from the government. A list of peaks opened for climbing by foreign expeditions is given in Appendix A. All foreign expeditions have to apply for permission to the Indian Mountaineering Foundation

(IMF). Details of the prescribed application form to obtain such permission is given in Appendix B, which also specifies the various conditions and the amounts payable in booking fees for peaks of different heights. These applications have to be sent through the Indian Mountaineering Foundation along with the application for permission to climb the peak. The IMF discourages expeditions with more than 12 members so as to curtail porters and mules, etc, which are difficult to discipline and adversely affect the environment as well as wildlife.

Mt. Hanuman (5366m) in Garhwal Himalaya has been classified as a trekking peak for foreign trekking parties. There is a separate set of prescribed application forms for obtaining permission from the IMF. The booking fee for this peak is US$ 400 at present and there will be no liaison officer deputed to accompany the party. The best season for climbing is May to October. The information on access contained in the Appendixes has been compiled through various circulars sent from the IMF. You *must* re-check with the IMF, *before* arrival in India, the latest rules in force about areas open for trekking and mountaineering.

Skiing

There is tremendous potential for cross-country skiing in the Garhwal Himalaya. Because of their height and range, the mountains here offer the thrill of exploratory long-distance skiing throughout the year. During winter cross-country runs from 5 to 20km are available, but are rather far from the roadheads. In 1978 the first ski descent was made from the summit of Mt. Trishul by two Italians. There is a ski resort at Auli, 12km from Joshimath, with basic infrastructure. The ski season at Auli is from mid December to March.

FISHING

Those who have travelled in the Garhwal initially associate the area with either trekking or Hindu pilgrimages. However, being a landscape dominated by numerous rivers it is also the haunt of the legendary mahseer. The mahseer (*Barbus tor putitora*) is present in many of the rivers that flow ultimately into the Bay of Bengal. Although in recent years the biggest fish have been caught on the Cauvery in southern India, the official record fish of 121lbs was caught in Assam on one of the tributaries of the Bramaphutra river.

51

The mahseer are handsome fish whose fast-flowing river environment makes them extraordinarily strong so that they put up a memorable fight when hooked. Their habitat - fast-flowing rivers that descend through spectacular mountain valleys in almost continual rapids - offers not only tremendous sport but also wonderful scenery and solitude. As ever, the best fishing tends to be in the most remote areas.

There are two periods of the year when anglers concentrate on mahseer fishing: in the autumn as the rivers begin to clear after the monsoon, and in the spring when the early monsoon rain begins to raise the level of the rivers again. Herein lies the first problem for anglers. There is no set date on which the rivers clear in the autumn; it all depends on the pattern of the rainfall in any particular monsoon. The Himalayan rivers clear from the west starting with the Sutlej, which may be clear as early as the beginning of September, whereas the Lohit, which is the easternmost tributary of the Bramaphutra, may not clear till mid November. The Garhwal rivers can be expected to clear around the end of September. In the spring the optimum fishing time can be even more variable, ranging in the Garhwal from the beginning of March to mid May. The timing of any angling trip is of paramount importance unless you have the time to simply 'sit it out' and wait for the river to clear.

The most enjoyable mahseer angling is to spin or lure fish for them. The rule 'big water-big fish-big tackle' applies. For the smaller rivers, a $1^1/2$ in spoon on 15lb b.s. line will be adequate but fishing the large river confluences will require 25lb b.s. line with much larger spoons. Spoons predominantly silver are most successful. Plugs are also used to great effect. Fish are taken on worm when the rivers are coloured and some anglers use a locally made flour/hempseed mixture.

With regard to tackle, my experience is that above all you need a rod and reel that are able to withstand the rigours of wading/falling in rocky rivers/forcing one's way along jungle-covered riverbanks. Modern carbon/boron fibre rods are not really tough enough to withstand the rough treatment they are liable to be subjected to; the best ones are undoubtedly the last generation of glass-fibre rods. Whether you use a fixed spool or level wind reel is largely a matter of personal preference, although I personally believe that a level wind provides the best control over the fish. A reel needs to hold not less than 150yds. Hooks of at least 4x strength are essential - lighter hooks will simply be straightened out on the first run a fish makes.

Where to fish presents something of a problem to any angler seeing the beautiful Garhwal rivers for the first time. The best venues tend to be where two rivers come together, especially if one river is clean and the other is coloured. Mahseer tend to sit in the coloured water waiting for their luckless prey to be washed by. Inevitably, as the rivers drop in the autumn, there is a great exodus downstream of all the fish population. A word of caution: while many of the river confluences are clearly the best places to fish, they are, unfortunately for the angler, also the site of Hindu shrines and as such it is not permissible to fish them.

The best known fishing venue in the Garhwal is without doubt the junction of the Nayar river and the Ganges at a place called Vyas Ghat. The confluence is some 16 miles downstream from Devapryag. The Nayar river clears much earlier than the Ganges and provides a really excellent opportunity to get into a big fish. In the early autumn the journey to Vyas Ghat has to be made from the south over the mountains via Kotdwara and Satpuli as any vehicular access from Deva Pryag will not be possible. The Mandakini and the Pindar rivers have tremendous potential for anglers but not at their confluence with the Ganges at Rudrapryag and Karapryag, which are both Hindu shrines on the main pilgrimage route.

Any angler would do well to read any of the famous old mahseer angling books before setting out on a trip; Thomas's *Rod in India*, *The Mighty Mahseer* by Skene Dhu or MacDonald's *Circumventing the Masheer* all contain a wealth of information and many practical tips - the fact that all the books were written over 50 years ago matters not a bit.

Alternatively, inspiration can be gained by visiting the Ganges at Laxchman Jhula above the town of Rishikesh. Here there is a suspension bridge over the Ganges for pedestrians wishing to cross the river to visit the ashrams. For generations the mahseer have been fed from the bridge by passing pilgrims. Standing on the bridge you can throw handfuls of peanuts into the river and see 20lb plus mahseer swimming effortlessly against the current, casually taking the offerings. If only angling were that simple!

The Kumaon is the region sandwiched between the Garhwal and Nepal border. Although geographically similar to the Garhwal region it is a far quieter area. This is mainly because, unlike the region dominated by the Ganges, the Kumaon rivers have mainly local religious significance. The most famous fishing venue in the Kumaon is Pancheswar. This is the junction of the Sarju river with the Kali river on the Nepal border. Many good fish are caught each year at Pancheswar. Unfortunately the accommodation at the junction leaves much to be desired and the area capable of being fished at the junction is relatively small. Because the Kumaon is generally a far more remote region than the Garhwal, any angler has to be prepared to travel long distances over mountain roads and camp on the riverside. The Kali is the largest river in the area which offers good fishing not only at Pancheswar but also at Tanakpur just above the barrage. The upper reaches of the river are remote but well worth visiting.

The junction of the Sarju and eastern Ramganga at Rameshwar is another well known mahseer location. Other rivers worth visiting include the upper reaches of the Purvi Nayar together with the western Ramganga and the Khosi near Corbett National Park. Fishing within the park is however not allowed.

Any angling trip to the Kumaon needs careful planning as well as careful timing. The smaller rivers will start to clear from the end of September with the larger rivers taking a further three weeks or so before they will produce worthwhile fishing.

As well as mahseer there are Himalayan Hill Trout (*Barilius Bola*) which provide good sport on both spoon and fly in the upper reaches of most rivers as well as in the lakes above the treeline. Some of the lakes also often hold very small Olive Carp which like the Kalabanse can be caught on various baits.

A local tour operator (Garhwal Adventure Pvt. Ltd, Rohini Plaza, Room No. 35, Second floor, 11-E Rajpur Road, Dehra Dun) has successfully arranged all my fishing tours in Garhwal and Kumaon.

RIVER RUNNING

Uttarakhand has excellent potential for river running. At present river running is concentrated mainly along the Ganges in the Rishikesh-Devprayag area. The Indian Association of Professional Rafting Outfitters (IAPRO), who have been commercially running rivers since 1987, in keeping with the objective of providing international standards of safety in the sport, have drawn up a set of safety and environment guidelines for river running. Life jackets and helmets are mandatory on all sections of the rivers for guests and guides both. IAPRO have explored several rivers for river rafting and operate river running expeditions in the following rivers. The trips last from 2 hours to a couple of days and can be booked either directly with the river rafting companies or through your tour operator.

1. *Upper Ganges river. Access from Rishikesh. Grade IV*
   Other than being the most sacred river in India the Upper Ganges is also the most popular white water river. Several outfitters operate semi-permanent camps between Devprayag and Rishikesh during the season - October to April. Short duration rafting and kayaking trips on the 70km stretch and longer multiday expeditions on its two tributaries, the Alaknanda and Bhagirathi rivers, are possible.

2. *Bhagirathi river. Access from Rishikesh - Tehri. Grade III/IV*
   The western tributary of the Ganges sports lively and continuous white water. A self-contained rafting expedition begins at Tehri for 4-5 days and joins the Ganges from Devprayag down to Rishikesh for 3 days, covering a total distance of about 140km. The Upper Bhagirathi near Uttarkashi is a Grade V run and ideal for kayaking. Season: October to April.

3. *Alaknanda river. Access from Rishikesh to Nandprayag. Grade IV+*
   The eastern tributary of the Ganges, Alaknanda, offers high-class white water and picturesque countryside for 120km between Nandprayag and Devprayag. Sections above Nand-prayag offer class V & VI great white water kayaking.

4. *Tons river. Access from Dehra Dun to Mori. Grade IV & V*
   One of the tributaries of Yamuna river, the Tons demarcates the borders of Himachal Pradesh and west Uttar Pradesh. The river flows through evergreen forest. Best season is May to June and September.

5. *Sarda river. Access from Tanakpur to Pancheshwar. Grade III & IV*
   The Sarda river in the north-east of Uttarakhand demarcating
   the border with Nepal offers about 100km of river running in a
   3 day self-contained expedition from Pancheshwar (confluence
   of the Sarda and Saryu rivers) up to the railhead at Tanakpur.

FLORA AND FAUNA

Most visitors to the region will of necessity approach from the
southern plains and will follow a tributary of the Ganges (Ganga)
through the foothills northward to the inner ranges. Whilst crossing
the Gangetic plain and still far from the foothills, there is a barely
discernible inclination to the land surface due to vast quantities of
sediment washed down from the rapidly eroding mountains. A
century and more ago, these alluvial fans bore the malarial, marshy
subtropical jungles known as the Terai. Now much depleted by
clearance for cultivation, the Terai nevertheless provides visitors
with their first impression of the vegetational changes which
accompany increasing elevation as they travel northwards.

On entering the foothills, the lower slopes, where not terraced or
reduced to pasturage, are also clothed in subtropical forest but at
around 1500-1800m (4900-5900ft) gradually yield to tree species
better adapted to temperate climates. Evergreen oaks,
rhododendrons and conifers predominate but many other tree
species and a variety of shrubs contribute to these temperate forests
which extend upwards to a limit of around 3700m (12,100ft). In
general, higher levels are attained by those forests on the colder,
wetter north-facing slopes which favour coniferous species, whereas
on the warmer, drier southerly faces the treeline is often lower due
to prevalence of the less hardy oaks and to burning for pasturage.
Above the treeline scrub-covered slopes, screes and rock outcrops
rise above alpine meadows to the zone of permanent ice and snow.
Although some valley glaciers descend to 3350m (11,000ft) the
snowline may be as high as 5800m (19,000ft) on some slopes in
summer and vegetation is commonly found up to 4800m (15,700ft).
For the majority of trekkers, however, who will visit during the
spring or autumn, the snowline may be substantially lower. This
threefold division of habitat into subtropical, temperate and alpine

serves as a framework within which to describe some of the floristic and faunal characteristics of the region which the casual visitor might expect to see during the spring or autumn. Those with specialist interest will need to refer to more authoritative texts (see Bibliography).

The subtropical zone is associated with one tree species perhaps more than any other, *Shorea robusta* (Sal), the most important hardwood source in the region. During April its large showy clusters of pale yellow flowers infuse the forest air with an intoxicating fragrance. Also abundant is *Bombax ciliata* (Silk-cotton Tree), closely related to Baobab and Balsa, which in early spring is resplendent with large scarlet flowers clustered on leafless branches. Of the 100 or so other tree species at this level *Dalbergia sissoo*, autumn-flowering *Mallotus philippinensis*, *Acacia catechu* and *Albizia chinensis* are abundant in lowland forest whilst on the ridges *Madhura indica*, the sweet sticky flowers of which are favoured by Sloth Bears, and the camelsfoot trees *Bauhinia racemosa* and *B. variegata* with their bilobed leaves and showy flowers are especially evident. The Indian Oleander, *Nerium indicum*, with its clusters of fragrant red, pink or white funnel-shaped blossoms and *Cassia fistula* (Indian Laburnum) clothed in bright yellow pea flowers also add vivid splashes of colour to the lower forests in springtime.

Most visitors to Garhwal and Kumaon (Uttarakhand) will probably be destined for the upper valleys and inner ranges and will not wish to linger in the lowland forests. It is, however, only here that many of the larger mammals may be seen and especially in those areas designated as national parks and reserves of which the Corbett National Park and Rajaji National Park (incorporating the Chila, Motichur and Rajaji wildlife sanctuaries) are the best known. Elephant and tiger, although not confined to these parks, are rarely seen elsewhere in Uttarakhand. Four species of deer, Sambar (*Cervus unicolor*), Swamp Deer (*Cervus duvauceli duvauceli*), Spotted Deer or Chital (*Axis axis*) and Hog Deer (*Axis porcinus)* also favour the Terai forests and are rarely found above the subtropical zone, as are also Sloth Bear (*Melursus ursinus*) and several animals which favour wetlands such as the rare Fishing Cat (*Felis viverrina*) and Clawless Otter (*Aonyx cinerea*). Lakes and rivers at this level are also the upper limit for Muggar or Marsh Crocodile (*Crocodylus palustris*), Gharial (*Gavialis gangeticus*), the long-snouted fish-eating crocodile, and several freshwater terrapins and turtles such as Indian Sawback (*Kachuga tecta*), Dhongoka Terrapin (*Kachuga dhongoka*), Brahminy Terrapin (*Hardella thurgii*) and Ganges Softshell (*Trionyx gangeticus*).

To see many of these animals requires perseverance and luck but this is less so for many of the butterflies of which there are some strikingly colourful species in the lowland forests. The Red Helen (*Princeps helenus helenus*), a large black swallowtail with red lunules and a yellowish patch on the hind wings, is common during both spring and autumn, gliding effortlessly through clearings. Others include the great Eggfly (*Hypolimnos bolina*), black with large blue patches, Common Tiger (*Danaus genutia*), orange with black veins and black and white apical areas, and the beautiful but scarce black-veined pale-blue Pale Wanderer (*Pareronia avatar avatar*).

Although the gaudy colours of some butterfly species are a warning to potential predators of their unpalatability, many are not so protected and may fall prey to the Redbreasted Falconet, a diminutive inhabitant of the Terai and forested foothills with a particular liking for these insects. Of the 600 or so other bird species in the subtropical zone many demand particular effort on the part of the visitor if they are to be seen but some are apparent to even the most casual observer. Babblers, of which the Jungle Babbler and Rufous-bellied Babbler are locally common, are often evident, usually in small flocks of six to twelve feeding noisily on the ground or flying in follow-my-leader formation low across paths, roads and forest clearings. In the spring, woodpeckers, of which there are many species in the Terai and wooded foothills, readily respond to human intrusion with loud warning calls. Often brightly coloured, they are nevertheless not necessarily easily seen. The Himalayan Goldenbacked Three-toed Woodpecker, the male of which has a crimson crown, crest and rump, is especially striking as is also the Large Yellownaped Woodpecker, a greenbacked species with a conspicuous golden yellow crest. A race of the Rufous Woodpecker, *ssp humei*, which is confined to Garhwal and Kumaon possibly extending into western Nepal, is locally common and often found feeding on the nests of tree ants. The male is frequently heard drumming furiously during the breeding season of April to June.

Also heard at this time is the powerful reverberating drumming of the Himalayan Great Slaty Woodpecker, a slate grey crow-sized bird with a buff yellow throat, an inhabitant of mature Sal forest.

Wild fig trees, of which there are several species fruiting in both spring and autumn, attract a variety of birds. Small flocks of Red-breasted Parakeets, noisy in flight, may be seen feeding silently on the fruit, their presence betrayed only by the rain of discarded debris. Pintailed, Wedgetailed and Orange-breasted Green Pigeons, which have a deceptively parrot-like gait and can cling to the underside of branches, also congregate in fruiting fig trees, their beautiful wandering whistling calls being the only clue to their presence.

In sharp contrast, during March to May, the incessant monotonous call of the Common Hawk Cuckoo resounds through the forest. As its shrieking high-pitched utterances sound like the avian rendition of *Brainfever* it is also known as the Brainfever Bird. A near relative, the Redwinged Crested Cuckoo, emits a similarly piercing harsh rasping scream and not content with daytime calls also produces a double whistling note at night. Another notable contributor to the daytime chorus is the Large Green Barbet, *ssp caniceps*, whose persistent metronomic call is soon echoed by others in the vicinity and is the best means of locating this pale green, brown-headed retiring bird. Early morning and late evening is the best time to see and hear the very shy Red Junglefowl and likewise the Peafowl, both of which are usually in small flocks of a single male and several females. Observant visitors may also glimpse the Shikra, a small rounded-winged hawk, ashy blue-grey above and barred below, which has the habit of ambushing small avian prey from a concealed perch, usually a tree adjacent to a clearing. The same hunting habit is employed by another forest species, the Crested Goshawk, and by the much larger Crested Serpent-Eagle which sits concealed in dense foliage at the top of a tall tree projecting above the canopy. It is more readily located when soaring, often at great height, and emitting its distinctive high-pitched whistling scream.

As most routes into the Himalayan foothills follow the broad river valleys known as dhuns, visitors will inevitably see some of the birds typical of freshwater habitats. During the period September to April two of the commonest species along the rivers at these lower altitudes are Plumbeous and Whitecapped Redstart, both altitudinal migrants which will be found breeding along mountain streams up to 4000m (13,100ft) from May to August. The Himalayan Pied Kingfisher, on the other hand, stays in the same low-level location, exceptionally up to 2000m (6500ft) throughout the year, as does also the Large Pied Wagtail, one of several wagtail species attracted to water but which in winter sometimes aggregates into nomadic flocks. Another species commonly seen along the lower rivers, although it can be found up to 3900m (12,800ft) when breeding, is the West Himalayan Brown Dipper, which like others of the same genus has the ability to feed underwater.

On entering the foothills, human intervention is no less apparent than in the lowlands, large areas having been clear felled and either terraced for cultivation or maintained as pasturage. Sufficient of the original vegetation remains, however, to suggest the composition and extent of the former forest cover which becomes progressively more evident as one ascends through the temperate zone, Garhwal and Kumaon having suffered less than many other parts of the Himalaya from uncontrolled deforestation.

Pinus roxburghii (Chir or Long-leaved Pine), which is tapped for resin and medicinal turpentine, forms extensive forests up to 2000m (6560ft) as do also several species of evergreen oak (*Quercus lanata. Q. leucotrichophora* and *Q. floribunda*) which are often associated with the widespread and abundant treeforming rhododendron *R. arboreum*, the blood red flowers of which colour the hillsides up to 2400m (7870ft). Above this level *Quercus semecarpifolia*, which may extend down to 2100m (6890ft), replaces the other oaks, usually accompanied by pink and white forms of *Rhododendron arboreum* and the red flowered *Rhododendron barbatum* up to 3600m (11,800ft), although locally the oak may extend up to the treeline. As *R. arboreum* flowers February to May and *R. barbatum* April to June, depending on altitude, those wishing to see the forest rhododendrons at their best should time their visit accordingly.

In the lower half of the temperate forests a species of birch, *Betula alnoides* with reddish papery bark, is locally common, its long slender female catkins a conspicuous feature of streamside stands during November and December. *Carpinus viminea*, a species of hornbeam, occupies similar well shaded waterside locations, whilst an evergreen relative of beech, *Castanopsis indica*, which produces creamy flowering spikes in October and November and an edible nut, locally forms extensive stands. Several trees of the Laurel family also occur in the lower oak forests. *Lindera pulcherrina* is common as a shrub in the understorey or as a large tree producing auxillary clusters of greenish-yellow flowers in March and April. *Neolitsea pallens, Persea odoratissima* and *Dodecadenia grandiflora* are other spring flowering species and *Cinnamomum tamala* the source of a substitute for cinnamon.

Human utilisation of the lower temperate forests is strikingly evident wherever there is settlement. Use of timber for construction and fuel, and foliage for animal feed and bedding is immediately apparent but there are many other less obvious uses which have a considerable influence on the composition of the flora. The cultivation of native and introduced bamboo is especially widespread. *Arundinaria falcata* and *Dendrocalamus hamiltoni* are the commonest low-altitude species, forming impenetrable thickets in the evergreen oak forests and near villages and used for making baskets and matting. *Dendrocalamus strictus*, on the other hand, is used for making implements, poles, scaffolding and charcoal for metalsmiths, whilst *Bambusa arundinacea*, a native of southern India and Burma, has been introduced for the value its great strength and size provide in construction. Willows are extensively planted for use in basket making and buildings, the species most commonly used being *Salix acmophylla, S. excelsa, S. alba* and *S. babylonica*. Of the indigenous species *S. disperma* is common along streamsides and provides toothbrushes from its terminal branches. The bark, leaves and young branches of *Cotinus coggyria* (Smoke Tree) are used in tanning and dyeing whilst *Lyonia ovalifolia*, a very abundant forest tree, is the source of an insecticide. Some forest trees provide timber for very specific purposes. That of *Fraxinus excelsior* (Common Ash) is used for making carts, whereas timber for ploughs is derived from *F. floribunda*, commonly planted around villages also for its beautiful springtime sprays of numerous white flowers.

Of the many flowering shrubs to be seen at lower levels many will be familiar as garden plants. *Cotoneaster microphyllus*, a mat forming shrub covered in small white flowers from May to June, is particularly common on pathside banks from 2000m (6560ft) upwards and is only one of many cotoneasters found in the region. The beautifully fragrant white clustered flowers of *Philadephus tormentosus* are also strikingly evident in wayside shrubberies during the same months as is also *Skimmia anquitilia* with its strongly aromatic leaves and terminal clusters of yellow flowers. Jasmins are well represented with *Jasminium multiflorum* common below 1500m (4900ft), its dense umbels of large white flowers appearing any time from March to October. Higher up *J. dispermum*, a woody climber with fragrant pink to white flowers appears, as does yellow-flowered *J. humile* and the showy *J. officinale* with its clusters of pink buds opening into large fragrant white flowers with pink corolla tubes, all spring to early summer flowering. Two species of privet also occur commonly in the oak forests and damp gullies: *Ligustrum compactum* has large terminal clusters of creamy white flowers and *L. indicum* much smaller clusters.

Mahonia acanthifolia, *Pyracantha crenulata* and *Berberis lycium* are other familiar species common along waysides and the large yellow flowers of *Hypericum oblongifolium* borne on woody stems arching from banks everywhere will be recognisable as a St. John's Wort. During spring and early summer months, honeysuckles, of which there are several species especially at higher altitudes, are in full flower. *Lonicera quinquelocularis*, perhaps the most abundant at lower levels, is particularly attractive to butterflies. Its creamy mildly scented flowers attract not only familiar species such as Indian Red Admiral (*Vanessa indica indica*) and Indian Tortoiseshell (*Aglais cachmirensis aesis*), both very common, but other more exotic species. The Hill Jezebel (*Delias belladona ithiela*), black with yellow spots on the undersides, white spots and a single yellow patch on the uppersides, is also common. Another large species, the Glassy Tiger (*Parantica aglea melanoides*), often seen on honeysuckle, has a transparent pale blue background to the wings heavily suffused with black on the veins and margins. A not infrequent visitor, although rarely seen at rest, is the Rose Windmill (*Atrophaneura latreillei*), a large dark red-bodied Swallowtail with red marginal lunules on the hindwings. Various Lycaenids (Small Blues), Hesperids (Skippers), Peirids (Whites and Yellows), Neptids (Sailers) and Precids (Pansies) also occur commonly at these lower altitudes.

Those visiting the Himalaya during the spring will understandably see a greater variety of flowering herbaceous plants than those who choose an autumn trek. This is particularly true of the valley routes which are invariably followed in passing through the temperate forest zone. Wayside banks in the spring are locally covered in the diminutive pale blue to white flowers of *Gentiana capitata* and *G. pedicellata*, the former extending to 4500m (14,760ft) and the latter 3800m (12,460ft). The white flowers of two strawberries, *Fragaria nubicola* which produces a globular fruit and *F. daltoniana*, a larger ovoid fruit but smaller flower, are also abundant in similar situations, often accompanied by lilac flowered *Viola pilosa* in profusion. A pale pink to white flowered dandelion-like composite *Gerbera gossypina* is common on slopes adjacent to pathways during the spring as is also a perennial Skullcap *Scutellaria scandens* which has spikes of pale yellow purple-lipped flowers. Steep well-shaped slopes in wet well-forested areas are locally covered in *Paeonia emodi* during May, the large ivory white-petalled flowers centred with a mass of orange-yellow stamens providing an eye-catching contrast to the dark deeply cut leaves.

Although many of the terrestrial and epiphytic orchids flower only during the summer monsoon months, there are a number of spring flowering species and a few which can be seen during the autumn. Most can only be located by searches of appropriate habitat although the casual observer may find a few of the commoner species adjacent to pathways. *Cephalanthera longifolia* (Sword-leaved Helleborine), a white flowered terrestrial species, is the most likely find during May to August although *Calanthe tricarinata* with spikes of pendant greenish-yellow, reddish-lipped flowers is locally common in forests from April to July. The related pink flowered *C. plantaginea* is less frequent. Epiphytic orchids must be searched for on the trunks and larger branches of moss and lichen laden trees although some also grow on mossy banks and wet rocks. Locally common species found in the oak-rhododendron forests between 1000-2000m (3280-6560ft) and flowering during March to June are *Coelogyne ochracea*, *C. cristata*, *Dendrobium amoenum* and *D. transparens*. All produce large (up to 9cm across in *C. cristata*) showy flowers in clusters or pairs, generally white with variously coloured markings. A noteworthy autumn flowering epiphytic orchid is the spectacular rose-pink flowered *Pleione praecox* which produces one or two 7-10cm diameter flowers on a short stalk.

Beyond the upper limits of intense cultivation which is around 2300-2500m (7550-8200ft) conifers assume dominance in the temperate forests. Some species such as *Cupressus torulosa* (Himalayan Cypress), which is confined to drier areas on limestone substrate at altitudes of 1800-3200m (5900-10,500ft), are very restricted in distribution. Others are much more widespread, forming very extensive forests, either mixed, as in the association of *Picea smithiana* (West Himalayan Spruce) with *Abbies pindrow* (West Himalayan Silver Fir) plus sometimes *Cedrus deodara* (Deodar) and *Pinus wallachiana* (Himalayan Blue Pine) or singly, for example *Abies spectabilis* (Himalayan Silver Fir) often dominant at 2800-4000m (9200-13,100ft) over large areas and *Tsuga dumosa* (Himalayan Hemlock) forming pure forests in the more humid valleys at 2100-3500m (6900-11,480ft). The coniferous cover is by no means uniform, however. *Quercus semecarpifolia* with or without the tree forming rhododendrons also forms extensive forests to the treeline and there are many tree species which extend their altitudinal range up the valleys well into the conifer's domain. Thus the maples *Acer sterculiaceum* and *A. candatum* are dominant species in some valleys up to 3500m (11,480ft) whilst *A. caesium* and *A. acuminatum*, the elm *Ulmus wallichiana* and *Aesculus indica* (Indian Horse Chestnut) are commonly found up to 3000m (9840ft). All are frequently lopped for animal fodder but when untouched their foliage provides some extraordinarily beautiful spring and autumn colour. Further variety in the tree cover at the uppermost limits is provided by *Betula utilis*, a medium sized birch with a distinctive bark which naturally peels away in pale translucent horizontal strips. Locally this forms extensive stands on slopes as does a willow *Salix denticulata*, both producing catkins in early spring. Two species of juniper, *Juniperus indica* in drier areas and *J. recurva* (Drooping Juniper), also form often extensive shrub-covered slopes from 2500m (8200ft) to the treeline whilst *Taxus baccata ssp wallichiana* (Himalayan Yew) is more usually found interspersed with other tree species in the forests or in shady ravines. In wetter areas a bamboo *Thamnocalamus spathiflora* is commonly found forming dense thickets from 2100-3600m (6900-11,800ft).

Shivling (Photo: Author)
Mt Hati and Ghori Parbat from Auli (Photo: Anup Shah)

Village children (Photo: Author)
Spinning thread on the trail (Photo: Author)

Of the wayside flowers visible in spring in the upper reaches of the forests several species of *Primula* are especially evident. Many more species flower during the summer monsoon months. *Primula denticulata* with its compact globular heads of purple to mauve-blue flowers on stout stems is particularly distinctive, often occurring in forest clearings and on banks in profusion although more abundant still on open slopes and alpine meadows above the treeline. An extremely variable species *P. edgeworthii*, which may be blue, lilac, pink or white flowered with a yellow centre bordered white, is locally common in the forests as is also pink flowered *P. petiolaris* which is nearly stalkless on a tight rosette of leaves. A lilac flowered species with obovate three-toothed petals, resembling *P. boothii*, is also abundant in the upper forests and lower meadows during April and May.

Another conspicuous flowering plant locally common on damp rock ledges is *Bergenia ciliata*, a member of the saxifrage family. The leafless arching stems bearing dense clusters of white, pink or purple flowers appear in the spring and the rounded leaves, which enlarge after flowering, turn bright red in the autumn. An orchid well worth searching for in the drier forested areas during May to June is one of the Lady's Slippers, *Cypripedium cordigerum*, which has very large solitary flowers with green or white spreading petals and sepals and a conspicuous white pouch-like lip. Also in the higher forests is one of the few terrestrial orchids flowering in the autumn, *Ponerorchis chusua* whose dark purple flowers appear from September to October.

At the upper limit of the forests conditions are sometimes favourable for extensive growth of a number of flowering shrubs which may only appear sporadically at lower altitudes. *Rhododendron companulatum* with bell shaped, pale mauve to rose-purple flowers in lax clusters, *Viburnum grandiflorum* which produces dense clusters of fragrant pink flowers on leafless branches and *Piptanthus nepalensis* with terminal clusters of large yellow pea flowers are especially evident during April and May at or near the treeline.

As most trekking routes through the temperate forests inevitably follow well established pathways used by local inhabitants, most of the larger mammals keep well away from such areas. Some species, however, such as Rhesus Macaque, the commonest monkey of

65

northern India, are attracted to human settlement and cultivation and so are frequently seen near villages and fields along such routes. The Common Langur, a long limbed black faced monkey with, in the Himalayan race, an almost white head and dark dense coat, is on the other hand only found in the forests well away from human activity. Usually in troops of 20 to 25 strong and found up to 3600m (12,000ft) they move with great agility through the trees when disturbed.

Two species of marten are known to occur in the region and being active day and night may be seen by observant visitors. The Beech or Stone Marten (*Martes foina*) inhabits the temperate forests from 1500m (5000ft) up to and well beyond the treeline and is a ceaseless hunter both in trees and on the ground. Its uniform brown coloration with white patches on the throat differentiate it from the other species, the Yellowthroated Marten (*Martes flavigula*) which is more varied in colour being dark brown, black and russet dorsally, with a markedly yellow throat. The Yellowthroated Marten is found from 2750m (9000ft) down to the subtropical zone and is exclusively arboreal, moving through the tree tops with astonishing speed and agility. The closely related weasels are represented in the area by four species, but being mainly nocturnal these are seldom seen. Similarly, two species of flying squirrel are nocturnal. Otters may sometimes be seen in daytime, the Clawless Otter near water in the foothills and the Common Otter up to 3600m (12,000ft). In areas of cultivation and scrub a subspecies of the Red Fox, *ssp montana*, known as the Hill Fox may be seen during daytime, as may also the Rufous-tailed Hare (*Lepus nigricollis ruficaudatus*) which although normally nocturnal is sometimes disturbed from its daytime resting place.

The Himalaya is the main centre of speciation for wild goats, sheep and the goat-antelopes, two of which, the Goral (*Nemorhaedus goral*) and Serow (*Capricornis sumatraensis*), can be seen in the temperate forests of this area. Goral favour elevations between 900 and 2750m (3000-9000ft) and can usually be seen early morning or late evening in small groups of four to eight feeding on rugged grassy hillsides. They are small stocky goat-like animals which in this region tend to be yellowish-grey suffused with black. Serow are usually found at altitudes between 1850-3050m (6000-10,000ft) and favour rocky slopes of thickly forested valleys where they feed morning and evening on grassy terraces, either singly or in small often widely dispersed groups of four to five. They are larger than Goral, much darker with pale lower limbs and being very wary are easily disturbed. Both species are best located by patient observation of suitable habitats with binoculars or telescope from a considerable distance.

Early morning and late evening are also the best times to see Barking Deer or Muntjac (*Muntiacus muntjak*) which often emerges either singly or in pairs to browse at the edge of dense forest. Their loud barking calls are usually heard at the same times or at night. Another species, the Musk Deer (*Morchus moschiferus*), a diminutive hornless animal with dark brown grey-speckled coat, is rarely seen although it does emerge to feed mornings and evenings from birch forest near the treeline. Other mammals known to occur in the temperate forests of Uttarakhand but rarely seen due to their nocturnal habits or secrecy include Tiger recorded up to 3050m (10,000ft), Leopard, Leopard Cat, Jungle Cat, Common and Himalayan Palm Civet, Indian Porcupine, Wild Boar, Jackal, Brown Bear and Himalayan Black Bear.

Trekking routes in the lower part of the temperate zone invariably pass through areas of cultivation and habitation where one of the most abundant birds in India, the Common Myna, is frequent. Dark brown with a black head, yellow bill and eye patch, it has conspicuous white wing flashes in flight. Also much in evidence in such areas is the Jungle Crow which can be seen anywhere near human habitation in the mountains, even up to shepherds' summer camps well above the treeline. Looking skyward one is also sure to see one or more Himalayan Griffon Vultures usually circling high on motionless wings or rapidly traversing the sky in a straight line with wings drawn in. Sometimes with them is Lammergeier or Bearded Vulture, which on permanently outstretched longer narrower wings is the most efficient flier of all. With its wedge-shaped tail, creamy white head and neck and orange chest produced by rubbing its feathers in iron oxides, it is an unmistakable bird.

Where routes run alongside rivers and streams, breeding Whitecapped and Plumbeous Redstarts and Brown Dippers will be seen during springtime. Grey Wagtails, the males of which have a conspicuous black bib and bright yellow underparts are also common, whilst Little and Blackbacked Forktails, black and white wagtail-like birds, although scarce, may be encountered on boulder strewn heavily wooded streams. Another species commonly seen near water although not necessarily confined to it is the Blue Whistling Thrush. Although Blackbird-like in appearance it has a beautifully flecked blue-purple plumage with white spots on the wings.

Of the hundreds of species which favour the temperate forests the magpies, tree pies and jays are amongst those most frequently seen. Red-billed and Yellow-billed Blue Magpies, both spectacularly colourful long-tailed blue-purple birds with black heads, are not only visually conspicuous but also advertise their presence with a remarkable vocabulary of loud, harsh calls, whistles and imitations of other birds. The Red-billed is usually found below 1600m (5250ft), the Yellow-billed above and up to 2700m (8850ft) when breeding during the spring but both move lower in late autumn. Of the tree pies, a race of the Indian Tree Pie, *ssp vagabunda*, is common in the forests up to 2000m (6560ft). A long-tailed bright rufous arboreal bird with a dark sooty grey head, it is often seen in pairs or noisy family parties associated with other birds which it follows around feeding on insects and fruit dislodged by them. The similar West Himalayan Tree Pie is equally abundant. Two species of jay, the West Himalayan Red-crowned and Black-throated, are also common and often seen together. Both prefer mixed pine, oak, rhododendron forest and can be located by their noisy calls.

There are many species of woodpecker in the forests, two of those most frequently seen being the Black-naped Green Woodpecker and the Scaly-bellied Green Woodpecker. The Black-naped is usually found up to 2400m (7870ft), has a high pitched musical call and is often seen on the ground feeding on ant and termite nests, whereas the Scaly-bellied is a tree feeder and has a wild ringing double note call. The males of both species drum during the springtime breeding season. Of the forest pigeons, the Speckled Wood Pigeon, a grey headed maroon coloured species with a speckled pale grey neck, is locally common but not easily located as it has the habit of staying absolutely motionless when alarmed, even when hanging upside down feeding on fruit trees.

Laughing thrushes, closely related to babblers, are well represented in the forest avifauna including Striated, Western White-throated and Variegated, all of which are locally common. The Striated Laughing Thrush is a light brown bird with strong white streaking and a pronounced crest, found up to 2700m (8850ft) in dense forest, feeding in the canopy. White-throated Laughing Thrush occurs from 1800m (5900ft) to the treeline in the spring and is often in small parties even during the breeding season. The Variegated Laughing Thrush found at similar altitudes is a very attractive multicoloured bird, overall tawny but with black facial markings, silvery-grey, chestnut and black and white wings and tail, and rufous belly. All three tend to aggregate into mixed feeding flocks in the autumn. Of the true thrushes, Grey-winged Blackbird and White-collared Blackbird are common, the males of both being all black with a pale grey wing patch in the former and a white collar and throat in the latter. The Grey-winged is one of India's finest songsters, the Black-collared less so, with a less varied mellow repertoire.

Other conspicuous forest species which one can reasonably expect to see include Verditer Flycatcher, Black-capped Sibia, Western Red-headed Tit, Rufous-bellied Crested Tit, White-browed Bush Robin and Grey or Ashy Drongo. Both Allied and Black and Yellow Grosbeak, two finches with massive bills, advertise their presence by calling repeatedly from the tops of conifers as does the Himalayan Nutcracker which is locally common around the treeline. One of the most spectacularly colourful of Himalayan birds, the Firetailed Sunbird, is also locally common at 3000-4000m (9800-13,100ft) where it feeds at *Rhododendron arboreum* and *R. campanulatum* flowers during the spring, descending to lower elevations by the autumn. With its scarlet back and tail extending into two long streamers, metallic purple and red head, olive wings and bright yellow underparts it is unmistakable. Equally distinctive but always difficult to observe in the forests are several species of pheasant of which the White-crested Kaleej, Koklas and Chir are all well represented. The Monal Pheasant is more easily seen as it inhabits the upper reaches of the forests and the scrub beyond the treeline, emerging into clearings and the open hillsides to feed. A male with its metallic azure blue, purple, green and bronze upper plumage, cinnamon rufous tail and velvety black undersides is an incomparable sight as it spreads its chestnut wings and fans its tail when displaying.

With increasing altitude the environmental pressures on plants and animals become ever more severe and in the Himalaya are further exacerbated by seasonal climatic changes. Most birds and mammals avoid the most extreme conditions of the alpine zone by altitudinal migration, moving to lower climes during the winter and returning to higher altitudes only in the spring or summer. Plants, however, must adapt to these extremes. Some of those described as occurring in the temperate forests extend their range beyond the treeline but there are many other species which are largely confined to the alpine zone.

Two species of rhododendron, *R. lepidotum* and *R. anthropogon*, are locally common above the treeline to 4800m (15,750ft), often covering steep slopes in dense low shrubberies which during May to July are enriched by clusters of variously coloured flowers. *R. anthropogon* is usually white or yellow tinged with pink whilst *R. lepidotum* may be pink, purple, or pale yellow. Also locally abundant on steep slopes are the ericacious shrubs *Gaultheria trichophylla* and *G. nummularioides* which form mats of minutely leaved woody stems often covering extensive areas. *G. trichophylla* produces tiny red, pink or white bells from May to July and numerous sky blue berries in the autumn, whereas the similar flowers of *G. nummularioides* appear later, during July to September, and the berries are black.

Meadows and grassy slopes above the treeline produce a succession of flowers as the winter snows retreat. Some of the earliest to appear are the white flowered anemones *A. biflora* and *A. rivularis*, the former tinged blue on the underside of the petals and the latter flushed violet. These and the yellow and bronze petalled composite *Oxygraphis polypetala* are usually present in profusion. Often in association are various species of *Primula* of which *P. denticulata* with its globular heads of purple to mauve-blue flowers is most abundant whilst hollows can be so dense with yellow *Gagea elegans* as to exclude all others species. With further retreat of the snows adjacent slopes may reveal some of the early flowering rock jasmines, exquisitely flowered plants which number amongst the most beautiful of all alpines. Of these, *Androsace lanuginosa* which produces compact pink or white umbels above silky haired leaf rosettes and *Androsace sarmentosa* with bright pink flowers, appear from May onwards up to 3900m (12,800ft). By June when slopes are beginning to clear to the permanent snowline, species such as *Androsace delavayi*, which is found up to 5200m (17,050ft) in Kumaon, appear. This is a cushion forming plant with tiny globular rosettes of minute silvery leaves and fragrant usually pure white flowers with greenish yellow throat.

During the autumn, pink flowered spikes of *Bistorta vaccinifolia* and *B. affinis*, arising from long trailing woody stems, cover the slopes in great swathes of colour. Gentians are also especially evident at this time. *Gentiana stipitata*, a pale blue to mauve tubular flowered species, can be found on stony slopes whilst stabilised screes are the preferred habitat of the deep blue cushion-forming *Gentiana tubiflora* which occurs from 4000-5000m (13,100-16,400ft). *Gentiana depressa*, a beautiful ice-blue green tinged bell flowered species, also occurs locally, often on exposed ridges and slopes, a location apparently also favoured by two species of edelweiss, *Leontopodium himalayanum* and *L. jacotianum*, both common between 3000 and 4500m (9850-14,750ft) from July to October.

Above the treeline there are few mammals which trekkers can reasonably expect to see. Constant vigilance aided by use of binoculars and an awareness of the habits and habitats of those animals which do occur can, however, greatly increase one's chances of seeing the more elusive species. One of the commonest and most frequently seen is the Mouse Hare, a guinea pig-like animal related to the hares, often found amongst rock outcrops and near large boulders under which it lives. Of the several species which occur in the Himalaya, *Ochotona roylei*, which in Garhwal and Kumaon is normally reddish brown with a pale band across the nape and occurs at 3400-4300m (11,150-14,100ft), is widespread, abundant and often very tame. Also locally common although confined to altitudes of 4000-5500m (13,100-18,000ft) is the Himalayan Marmot, a large rodent related to the squirrels, living colonially in burrows where they hibernate during the winter. Although extremely wary, they can sometimes be seen feeding near their burrows before the piercing whistle of a lookout sends them scurrying underground for safety.

Of the Himalayan wild goats and sheep, three species occur above the treeline in the Garhwal-Kumaon region; the Bharal or Blue Sheep (*Pseudois nayaur*), Ibex (*Capra ibex*) and Himalayan Tahr (*Hemitragus jemlachicus*). All three live in herds although older males move away in late summer and return in the autumn for the rut, young being born the following spring. Bharal winter near the treeline and move up with the retreating snow to an altitude of 4880m (16,000ft) by mid summer and should be looked for on grassy slopes and terraces where they feed and rest throughout the day. Ibex are adapted to survive the most extreme climatic conditions and are usually found at or above the snowline, descending only in the spring to avail themselves of fresh grazing. They feed early morning and late evening never far from the security of precipitous cliffs and crags which they climb with ease. The Himalayan Tahr chooses the most inaccessible terrain available, usually at altitudes of 2500-4400m (7200-14,400ft) in areas of dense scrub and forest adjacent to towering cliffs which they climb with an ability which surpasses even that of the Ibex. As they also favour shelter and shade, they are the most elusive of all the Himalayan goats, mature males especially being rarely seen.

Of the other large mammals occurring in the alpine zone, Brown Bears although predominantly nocturnal may sometimes be seen near the snowline in early spring, females with young cubs especially needing to feed for as long as possible soon after emerging from hibernation. They uproot large areas of turf and overturn many rocks in search of bulbs, rhizomes, roots, insects, larvae and small rodents. During the autumn they descend to feed on the fruits and berries of the forests before returning to hibernate at higher levels. Himalayan Black Bears, on the other hand, seldom ascend much above the treeline, being predominantly forest animals, and are also active mainly at night so sightings by visitors are infrequent. The extremely elusive Snow Leopard, which although occuring up to 4000m (13,100ft) during the summer and known to occur in the region, is again mainly nocturnal and therefore very rarely seen.

Birdlife in the alpine zone is limited in both numbers and variety but nevertheless includes some interesting species. Especially evident in areas where there are suitable caves for nesting are flocks of Alpine or Yellow-billed Chough often accompanied by the cliff-nesting Red-billed species at lower altitudes. Rocky boulder strewn terrain everywhere up to 4800m (15,750ft) will be occupied by breeding pairs of Black Redstart during the spring. The male with its grey crown and mantle, rufous underparts and rump, black throat and chest is especially evident when on territory, flying nervously from rock to rock. The even more colourful black, white and chestnut Guldenstadt's Redstart is far less common but can be found amongst rocky meadows and along glacial streams up to 5200m (17,050ft) from April to September. Alpine meadows and grassy slopes near melting snow are the preferred habitat of Vinaceous-breasted Pipit, a common summer visitor which is seen as breeding pairs in May but by early September is aggregating into large flocks of adults and juveniles preparing for migration. Several species of accentor and rosefinch also adopt this flocking habit during the autumn, often in mixed assemblages of more than one species. The often remarkably tame Garhwal Alpine Accentor inhabits stony slopes, rock outcrops and cliffs when breeding and the Western Rufous-breasted Accentor is a common but retiring species of juniper and willow scrub. They are grey-brown Hedge Sparrow-like birds with rufous underparts, attractively flecked with white and black. Both the Pink-browed Rosefinch and Indian Rosefinch are common up to 4000m arriving to breed during June and July and leaving in September. They frequent willow, juniper and birch scrub but are most often seen when busily feeding in large flocks on the ground. The Pink-browed is especially common in upland villages during the winter from November to April. A third species, the Garhwal Dark Rosefinch, is an uncommon and little known bird of stony pastures near the treeline.

Two species of pigeon, the West Himalayan Snow Pigeon and Turkestan Hill Pigeon, can be seen by those visiting during spring or autumn. Except when breeding they are usually in large flocks, those of the Hill Pigeon commuting between their high altitude cliff roosts and cultivated feeding grounds both morning and afternoon whereas the Snow Pigeon feeds on hillsides often near melting snow. Both are seen in pairs or small groups during the summer and retire in large flocks to cultivations at lower altitudes during the winter. Although they appear black and white in flight only the Snow Pigeon has a black head, that of the other species being grey.

Bare stony hillsides with sparse scrub is the preferred habitat of Chukor, one of several partridges and related species which breed in the alpine zone. The loud ringing call of the male is the best guide to their location in springtime, otherwise they are not easily seen unless disturbed into flight from their ground cover. The closely related Snow Partridge favours hillside with more extensive scrub cover close to the snowline whereas the much larger Himalayan Snowcock, a handsome grey and white bird streaked and chestnut, buff and black, is found on bare stony ridges at 4000-5000m (13,100-16,400ft), only descending to the treeline in severe winters. All three are most likely to be seen in pairs or small parties during the spring, aggregating into larger coveys of twenty or more in the autumn.

NATIONAL PARKS

Corbett National Park

The park, named after the famous naturalist Jim Corbett, is situated partly in Garhwal and partly in Nainital district. It has an area of 525sq km, altitude 250m/900ft to 1100m/3600ft. The park is closed from about mid June to mid November. It is the oldest National Park in India and one of the best for the typical big mammals of northern India. Main wildlife species found are tiger, elephant, panther, sloth, deer, cheetal, sambhar, wild boar, monkey, porcupine, mongoose, crocodile, goral and over 500 species of bird.

How To Get There: Nearest railhead at Ramnagar is 52km from Dhikala, the base for viewing wildlife. From there public buses and taxis are available to Dhikala. It is 290km by road from Delhi, 240km from Lucknow, capital of Uttar Pradesh, 106km from Nainital, 112km from Ranikhet and 255km from Dehra Dun. Taxis, public buses and chartered buses can be hired from all these places for Dhikala. Transport within the park can be chartered from the Wild Life Warden, Corbett National Park, Ramnagar District, Nainital. Riding elephants to view the wildlife are available for hire.

Accommodation: There are forest rest houses, cabins, log huts, cottage tents and caravan platforms for camping. In addition to this, at Dhikala there are 2/3-room rest houses at Khinanauli, Sultan, Kanda, Malani, Jhirna, Bijrani, Paterpani, Gairal and Sarapduli. There are also very good hotels at several places bordering the park.

There are a few luxury hotels outside the park where reservations can be made in advance through tour operators.

Reservation Of Accommodation: Against advance payment through tour operators or one of the following:

i.   Field Director, Project Tiger, Ramnagar District, Nainital (U.P.).

ii.   Chief Wildlife Warden, U.P., Lucknow.

iii. U.P. Tourist Office, Chandralok Building, 36 Janpath, New Delhi.

Rajaji National Park

In 1983 three wildlife sanctuaries - Chila, Motichur and Rajaji, an area of 820sq km - were consolidated into one to promote the conservation of wild life. It spreads out to the Shivalik hills of Dehra Dun, Garhwal and Saharanpur districts. Dehra Dun and the sacred towns of Hardwar and Rishikesh are located in the immediate surroundings of the park, which is closed from 15th June to 10th November. Wildlife in the park includes elephants, tigers, leopards, Himalayan yellow-throated marten, various species of deer and antelope, Civet cat, wild boar, langur and monkey. Visitors have a very good chance of seeing spotted deer, sambhar, barking deer, nilgai, ghoral and several bird species, including peacock. The park altitude varies between 302m / 1020ft and 1000m / 3500ft and visiting hours are sunrise till sunset. Use of radios, loudspeakers, tape recorders, transistors, carhorns, spot lights, photo flashlights etc. are prohibited in the park, as well as in Corbett National Park. No one is permitted to sleep outdoors in the park.

How To Get There: The park is accessible by rail and road from Hardwar, Dehra Dun, Delhi and Lucknow. The entry gates at Mohand and Ranipur are only 5 to 6 hours' drive from Delhi by road. The Park has five entrances:

1.   Mohand, 25km from Dehra Dun on the Delhi-Dehra Dun road.

2.   Ranipur, 9km along the Hardwar-BHEL-Mohund road.

3.   Motichur, 9km from Hardwar on the Hardwar-Rishikesh road.

4.   Chilla, 9km from Hardwar on the Rishikesh-Kotdwar road (promising wildlife).

5.   Laldhang, 25km from Kotdwar on the Kotdwar-Chila road.

Accommodation: Best accommodation in the park is at Chilla with three rooms at the Forest rest house, a tourist bungalow and a tented camp with meal facilities. At other places there are two-room forest rest houses. Reservations for the rest houses are made from the Director, Rajaji National Park, 5/1 Ansari marg, Dehra Dun-248001. Day return trips can be made from comfortable hotels at Dehra Dun and Rishikesh.

Other National Parks

With a view to protecting ecologically fragile areas and to promote conservation of the wildlife and their habitat, certain other areas have been designated National Parks. Wildlife in these parks is rarely seen and they are therefore not listed in this guidebook.

Temples

To some the Himalaya is the land of gods where spiritual solace can be sought. To others it may be the theme for a painting, poem or song, an ideal place for a relaxed holiday or a challenge to an adventurer. Hindu mythology prescribes 'Yatra', or pilgrimage, to places of religious importance for salvation. It is believed that a true devotee is tested for kindness by God in cognito. This explains the presence of a large number of beggars in religious places, where they can receive, with some respect, food and clothes from the devotees. The modern motorised pilgrimage has tremendously increased the pressure on temples, and tourists, even non-Hindus, have started taking an interest in the temples.

Before describing some of the important temples of Uttarakhand, it is important to caution readers that the religious sentiments of all faiths must be respected. Shoes are taken off before entering a temple. Non-vegetarian food and alcohol are not allowed on temple premises and in certain religious towns such as Hardwar, Rishikesh, Badrinath, Kedarnath, Gangotri and Yamunotri. Displays of affection are not allowed in public. There are no restrictions on what clothes may be worn. Photography is not allowed inside the temples and at public bathing places near temples. For religious persons who have the means to visit all the four most sacred shrines of Uttarakhand in one go, the prescribed sequence is Yamunotri, Gangotri, Kedarnath and Badrinath. One can, however, visit any temple of choice.

TEMPLES IN GARHWAL
Badrinath

The temple situated on the right bank of Alaknanda river in the middle of an open valley at 3120m/10,300ft is among the most sacred of Hindu temples. Mt. Nilkanth, 6597m/21,640ft, dominates the temple and provides a very beautiful setting. It is dedicated to Vishnu, the preserver in Hindu mythology. The Shankaracharya set up four very important temples including Badrinath around the eighth century in the four corners of the country to revive the Hindu religion, which had received a setback owing to the propagation of

Budhism. Dwarka, Puri and Rameshwaram are the other three.

The idol in the principal temple is formed of black stone and stands about 3ft high. It is clothed with rich gold brocade and adorned with many gold and silver ornaments. Above its head is a small golden canopy (Chhattar). In front are several ever-burning oil lamps. To the right of the idol are the images of Nar and Narayana and on the left those of Kubera and Narda. Only the chief priest, the 'Rawal', can touch the idol of Vishnu.

A short distance below the temple is the bathing tank, connected to a hot water spring by a spout in the form of a dragon's head. There are separate bathing places for men and women. A devotee bathes in the icy cold water of Naradkhund first if he can, and then in the hot water tank, called 'Taptkund', before visiting the temple.

The Rawal is always a Namboodripad brahmin from Kerala state. He is appointed by a temple committee which also runs the administration of the temple. The chief executive officer of this committee is a civil servant appointed by the government of Uttar Pradesh. There are several local priests in the temple who are assigned different responsibilities. They enjoy semi-hereditary appointments.

Hindus perform different rituals for birth, death, thanksgiving, etc. These rituals are performed with the assistance of a priest or 'Panda' at all the main temples. The service at Badrinath is provided by a Brahmin community from Devprayag who provide a very efficient service to the pilgrims and assist them in every possible way, including finding accommodation. The Panda is paid a negotiated fee for the services.

The temple opens on an auspicious day in early May when the snow starts melting, the exact date decided by the temple committee and astrologers. People come in large numbers on this day to attend the flame viewing ceremony. The flame is kept burning in the temple when it is closed for the winter. At the closing ceremony in November the deity is covered with a woollen garment (Choli) specially woven by unmarried girls of the Malapa families of Mana village. This Choli is taken off the deity on the opening day of the temple and small pieces of it are distributed to pilgrims as blessings, called 'Mahaprashad'.

Offerings at all temples, including Badrinath, may be in the form of cash, ornaments, dried fruits, flowers, etc. in varying quantities depending on individual capacity, the cash and ornaments being placed in a sealed box. This constitutes the main income of the temple. Other offerings, which can be purchased from shops close to the temple, are placed on a plate which is put before the deity, then given back to the devotee by the priest. The devotee takes the contents home for distribution to family members and friends as 'Prashad', or blessings, of the deity, then returns the plate to the shopkeeper.

Regular prayers performed by the Rawal at around 6am and 6pm are very important ceremonies. Anyone, irrespective of religious faith, can attend the prayers. The temple remains open for visitors during the day except for about 3 hours in the afternoon.

The main religious and other places in and around Badrinath are:

The Panch Shilas (Five Stones): Around the Tapt kund (hotwater tank) there are five conspicuous stone slabs which according to Hindu mythology are:

1. *Narad Shila:* It stands between Tapt kund and Narad kund and is conical in shape. The sage Narad is believed to have meditated on this stone.

2. *Narsingh Shila:* A huge stone resembling the jaw and claws of a lion stands in the Alaknanda river, just below Narad Shila. Narsingh, incarnation of Vishnu, is believed to have stayed on this stone for a while to cool himself after killing the demon king Hiranyakshyap. The incarnation is a combination of man (Nar) and lion (Singh).

3. *Barah Shila:* Near Narsingh shila, it has the shape of a boar. (Barah is another incarnation of Vishnu).

4. *Garur Shila:* Near Tapt kund. According to legend Garur, the carrier of Vishnu, is believed to have meditated on this stone and now lives in the form of the stone.

5. *Markandey Shila:* It is believed that the sage Markandey meditated on this stone and attained heaven. The stone is in the Alaknanda river and is not visible in summer or during monsoons.

Shesh Netra: On the left of the Alaknanda, below Nar Parbat and between the two monsoon pools with lotus growing in them, is a large stone with a mark resembling an eye of Sesh Nag (Cobra) and called Shesh Netra (eye).

Charanpaduka: 2km uphill from the temple. It is said that Lord Vishnu descended here from heaven and slept on this large stone. It has footprints believed to be of Vishnu.

Mana Village: The last village in the valley, 3km north of Badrinath. Foreigners are not allowed to go beyond Badrinath town in this direction. It is believed that ancestors of the Mana people lived near Tehri and fled to Tibet to escape the wrath of the Maharaja of Tehri who was angry with them. After some time they returned to Garhwal but settled in Mana, a safe distance away from Tehri. These people were known as 'Marchhas' (goatsmen) because they carried their merchandise on goats. They did flourishing business with Tibet until about 1960. With the occupation of Tibet by China, trade links between India and Tibet were severed.

Mata Moorti: A small temple opposite Mana village, across the Alaknanda. It is believed to have the power of granting renunciation to those who meditate at the temple with a wish to renunciate their attachment with home and earth. It is also believed to bring back to the family fold the wayward children of parents who worship here.

Vyas Gufa (cave): There are several caves near Mana village and some of them, such as Ganesh Gufa and Bhim Gufa, are associated with saints and sages. The Vyas Gufa, under a huge rock, looks like a book and is called Vyas Granth (religious book). It is believed that Maharishi Vedvyas wrote the epic *Mahabharata* in this cave. A marble statue of Ved Vyas showing him writing is placed here.

The Saraswati: This river is dedicated to the goddess of learning. It originates from a glacier north of Mana. It is believed that Ved Vyas was blessed by the Saraswati to write the *Mahabharata*.

Bhimpul (Bhim's bridge): A huge stone bridging the Saraswati, near Mana, believed to have been placed over the river by mighty Bhim, one of the Pandava brothers of the epic *Mahabharata*. It provides a spectacular view of the roaring river.

Vasudhara Falls: 3km beyond Mana village towards the west is the captivating 145m high Vasudhara Falls in a perfect setting with Mt. Satopanth and Chaukhamba behind. The waterfall, reduced virtually to spray and swinging in the direction of the wind, can give the impression that it has stopped flowing.

Laxmivan: 4km from Vasudhara Falls and consisting of a birch groove where Laxmi, the goddess of wealth, is believed to have meditated.

Alakapuri (source of the Alaknanda): 3km further on from Laxmivan and 15km from Badrinath, at a height of about 4000m.

Chakratirth: 9km from Laxmivan, adjoining the ridges of Nar and Narayan peaks with several water channels flowing through the meadows. It is believed that Arjuna, of the *Mahabharata* epic, acquired the power to defeat Kauravas by bathing and meditating here.

Satopanth lake: 4km north of Chakratirth is the triangular-shaped Satopanth lake, at 4402m. The three corners of this 1km circumference glacial lake are believed to be the abodes of Brahma (creator), Vishnu (preserver) and Shiva (destroyer), the three supreme powers. Bathing in this lake on the eleventh day of solar and lunar fortnights is considered most auspicious.

Beyond Mana, one needs to be fully equipped and self supporting and, for the present, foreigners are not allowed in this area. However, its temples are listed here to explain the legends.

Kedarnath

This temple, dedicated to Shiva (the destroyer), stands near the head of the valley of Mandakini at 3583m/11,800ft on the banks of the Mandakini river. The legend goes that the invisible form of Shiva, fleeing from the Pandavas and not wanting to bless them after the battle of Mahabharata, took refuge here in the form of a bull and dived into the ground, showing the hind part on the surface. The Pandavas worshipped this hump as Lord Shiva and everyone followed the practice. This ancient temple, renovated and established, like Badrinath, by Shankaracharya, is built of large, evenly cut grey stones. It has a Garva Griha (sanctum sanctorium) to perform prayers. It is built on flat, grassy land directly below the Kedarnath and Bhartekunta peaks. It is a spectacular site with Nandi bull (Shiva's Mount), made from a huge rock, in front of the temple. Prayers are conducted in the temple in the mornings and evenings.

Places of religious significance in and around Kedarnath are the Hans kund, Udak kund, Rat kund and Bhaironnath temple, which is believed to protect the region when the Kedarnath temple closes for winter. Chorabari lake or Gandhi Sarovar, about $1^1/2$km from the temple, is a pretty glacial lake at about 3900m/12,200ft on the way to the Mt. Bhartekunta base camp. Another pretty lake abut 5km away above the right bank of the Mandakini is Vasukital. About 4km from the temple, on the way to the Mahapanth peak, is a precipice known as Bhairon Jhap. In ancient days devotees used to jump to their death from Bhairon Jhap believing it to be a sure way to reach heaven.

Trek To Kedarnath:
Kedarnath is connected by a 14km mule trek to the roadhead at Gaurikund, 1982m. One must leave Gaurikund before 6am to avoid the strong sun on the uphill trek. The well-made trail rises gradually but is rather narrow in places; ponies also use the trail. Be careful to keep in to the hillside while passing the ponies, which tend to keep to the edge. A nudge from a pony can throw a person several feet below the ridge. The path is through narrow valley and forest for the first 10km.

There are tea houses every 3-4km serving hot tea, cold drinks and snacks. The path is dotted with small temples and the temporary shelters of Sadhus and beggars where you can receive blessings after placing some money, usually 25 paise to a rupee, at a place conspicuously marked! You come across devotees returning from Kedarnath. The common form of greeting is "Kedarnathji ki jai" (Hail, the deity Kedarnath). Passing through jungle chatti, you reach Rambara, a big village with several eating places and almost midway. If you are not carrying a picnic lunch this is a good place to eat. You can find some shelter here for the night.

From Rambara the trail is steeper but prettier. In May many places will have several feet of avalanched winter snow through which a path is cut by the public roadbuilders and maintained during the season. From Garur Chatti the path is through a much wider valley and an easy gradient. If you are not acclimatised, your progress may be very slow or you may suffer from the usual headache. Keep moving slowly and do not forget to wear headgear. It will help to keep cold and headache under check.

The temple of Kedarnath is a gorgeous recollection of legend, myth and history, profusely embroidered with carvings. Set in a panorama of dominating Mt. Kedarnath and Bhartekunta, a visit to the temple is an awe-inspiring experience.

Panch Kedars

It is said that when Shiva dived into the ground at Kedarnath in the form of a bull, leaving his hind parts on the surface, his arms (Bahu) appeared at Tungnath, his face at Rudranath, belly at Madmaheshwar and head at Kalpeshwar. These together are called Panch (five) Kedars. The front of the bull is believed to have appeared at Pashupatinath temple in Kathmandu, Nepal. All these temples are dedicated to Shiva.

Tungnath: The temple is situated at 3640m / 11,500ft providing great views of the Kedarnath range of peaks and is on the Kedarnath-Gopeshwar-Badrinath motor road via Ukhimath and Chopta from where it is a 3km trek on a very well made path. There is a priest to help offer prayers at the stone temple.

Rudranath: Situated at 2296m / 8050ft in a meadow overlooking the Mt. Nandadevi range. Rudranath is reached by a 17km trek from Gangolgaon village, 3km short of Gopeshwar on the road from Ukhimath or Chopta. It is an uphill trek through forest via Panar and Naila shepherd huts.

Kalpeshwar: In the picturesque Urgam valley, which is reached from Rudranath by a 36km forest trek via Dumak, Kimana and Palla shepherd huts. It is a very pretty route, at an altitude of 2200m to 2140m. A local guide is recommended to take you through several goat paths. From Urgam, the roadhead at Helong is 9km along the route to Joshimath, 14km further on.

Madmaheshwar: On the Kedarnath road linked by a 13km road to Kalimath from Guptkashi. The main temples of Mahakali, Mahalakshmi, Shiva and Bhairab at Kalimath, 1463m / 5200ft. Apart from the religious significance of the place to a large number of devotees, the entire trekking route is of scenic beauty providing lovely mountain views of Chaukhamba and the Kedarnath ranges.

Gangotri

Situated at 3140m on the right bank of Bhagirathi river is the Gangotri temple built early in the 19th century. According to legend, as a result of the curse of a great saint, Kapil, ancestors of King Bhagirath were burnt alive at this spot and could reach heaven only if the Ganga could be brought down from heaven to touch the bones of the dead. Their grandson King Bhagirath meditated at this spot for several years and the Ganga was thus brought down from heaven to touch the ashes of the dead. They rose to life and attained heaven. The Ganga is called Bhagirathi, after King Bhagirath, until it joins the Alaknanda at Devprayag about 200km further down. It is believed that by bathing in this river and drinking the water all sins are washed away and the devotee attains heaven at the end of life. It is also believed that the water from Bhagirathi Ganga is never contaminated. Hindus worship Ganga as a sacred river and refer to her as 'mother' for it protects them. Scientists attribute the non-contamination of Bhagirathi waters to the minerals and medicinal properties in the Gangotri glacier, the source of the river. Perhaps the snout of the glacier must have been at Gangotri thousands of years ago as the name 'Gangotri' (Ganga descends) suggests. With the receding of the glacier the source has now moved 18km upwards to a place called 'Gaumukh' (Mouth of Cow), although it does not at all resemble the mouth of a cow.

The Gangotri temple is a square building about 20ft high situated in the midst of giant rocks. Inside are statues of Ganga, Bhagirath, Saraswati (goddess of learning), Laxshmi (goddess of wealth) and Annapurna (meal provider). The male villagers of Mukhwa act as Pujaris (priests) and Pandas (helpers to pilgrims).

Administration of the temple is in the hands of a committee elected from the villagers of Mukhwa, Dharali and saints living in Gangotri with a senior revenue official called Tahsildar as representative of the government. One of the priests acts as secretary of the committee.

The temple opens on an auspicious day in the last week of April or in early May. It closes for winter with great ritual in November on the day of the Festival of Lights, called Diwali. The devotees take a holy dip in the freezing waters of the sacred Ganga before offering prayers at the temple. Before departing, they carry jars of water from the Bhagirathi as the Prasad (blessings) of mother Ganges. Back home this water is distributed in drops to family members and friends to drink.

There are Dharamshalas, inspection houses and tourist bungalows for accommodation and several simple eating places. It is a great experience to visit the hermitages of several saints and to talk to them. All mountaineering expeditions and trekking parties to the Gangotri glacier region, Kedartal and Rudugaira start from Gangotri. The Bhagirath Shila, just outside the temple, and Gaurikund where the Bhagirathi makes a spectacular 20ft fall then flows through a narrow gorge lined with hard rocks, must not be missed. Gangotri can be reached in one day from Rishikesh by public bus, taking about 11 hours, via Tehri and Uttarkashi. You can use Gangotri as a base for 3-4 days from where a trek to the source of the Ganges and other nearby places, such as Kedartal and Patangnidhar-Rudugaira, can be enjoyed. Giant Deodar (cedar) trees in the Bhagirathi valley from Harsil onwards are a great sight. 9km short of Gangotri is a magnificent bridge built over the Janavi river (Jad Ganga). It is 450ft high and links Lanka with Bhaironghati. Lanka is a starting point for a route into Tibet, via Nilang, though no-one is allowed to enter Nilang itself. There are over a dozen peaks including Mt. Bhagirathi group, Shivling, Meru, Kharcha Kund, Matri, Thelu, Rudugaira and Kedarnath. From here you can also trek to Badrinath, via the Kalindikhal pass, with a permit from the District Magistrate at Uttarkashi.

Yamunotri

Yamunotri is in Uttarkashi District on the western flank of Mt. Bandarpunch at an elevation of 3323m/10,400ft and about 6km below the Kalind Parbat glacier from which the Yamuna or Jamuna river flows. It is believed that the god of fire (Agni Dev) meditated here, which caused hotwater springs to emerge. The temple is situated on the left bank of the Yamuna on a steep hillside. The idol of Yamuna is made of black marble. The hotwater springs close by have been channelled into tanks to facilitate bathing. Devotees put into the boiling water (Surya Kund) some rice and potatoes tied loosely in a cloth and in a few minutes it is cooked. It is then taken home by the devotees for distribution to family members as blessings

(Prashad) of the deity. There is a stone of divine light called Divya Shila which is also a place of worship. The priests or Pandas working in this temple belong to Kharsali village. The temple opens on an auspicious day in early May and closes on the day of Diwali or Festival of Lights.

To reach the temple you have to drive to Hanuman chatti, a day's drive from the railhead at Dehra Dun/Rishikesh or Uttarkashi. The last 13km are a trek on a well made path. There is no accommodation at Yamunotri for pilgrims so devotees have to return to Jankibaichatti or Hanuman chatti for the night, where simple accommodation and eating houses are available. Those who do not wish to trek have the option to hire a pony, or Kandy, to get to Yamnotri from the roadhead. Porters are available to carry baggage. There is a demanding but interesting trekking route from Janki chatti to Harkidoon over a 4500m pass. A visit to Yamunotri itself is not, however, as scenic as other pilgrim centres.

Devprayag
This town is at the confluence of the Alaknanda and Bhagirathi rivers in the district of Tehri at 472m elevation, 70km from Rishikesh. From here the two holy rivers unite to become the Ganga, the life giver, bringing salvation to the devout who gather in the religious fervour on her shores across the plains of northern India through to its outlet into the Bay of Bengal, called Ganga Sagar. The great temple of Raghunath, built of massive uncemented stone blocks, stands on a terrace in the upper part of the town together with the 6ft tall image of Lord Vishnu, made of black granite. A holy bath is taken by devotees at the junction of these two rivers. The bathing place on the Alaknanda is known as Vashishtkund, and on the Bhagirathi as Brahm kund. The confluence of the two rivers and the town above provides a picturesque setting. Devprayag is en-route to the Badrinath and Kedarnath shrines 67km from Rishikesh. Apart from Dharamshalas there is also a tourist bungalow with several eating places and shops selling the daily needs of Indian travellers and villagers. The Pandas of Badrinath belong to this town, some of whom are learned astrologers and priests of repute.

TEMPLES IN KUMAON

There are several temples in Kumaon which, though not of the magnitude of Badrinath or Gangotri, nevertheless have their own importance for religious people. For example, the Nandadevi temples in several towns and villages are dedicated to the goddess Nanda, otherwise known as Parvati, consort of Shiva. Details of some of the temples have been given in the section on the hill stations of Kumaon and there are a few more well-known shrines at Bageshwar, with Bagnath temple constructed in 1602 AD. An annual Uttarayan fair is held here in mid January, which is visited by thousands of people from far and near. In Jageshwar there is a group of 124 exquisitely stone-carved temples on the Almora-Pithoragarh road. During a big annual fair held in March / April, devotees take a holy dip in the Brahma kund dedicated to Shiva. On the same route is the Chaumu temple at Pancheshwar, at the confluence of the Kali and Saryu rivers. The Punyagiri temples are at Purmagiri, a small hilltop on the banks of the Kali on Tanakpur road. The Baijnath temples, 19km from Kausani on the banks of the Gomti, date back to the 12th century. Their intricate carving and stonework is awe-inspiring.

ACCESS ROUTES BY TRANSPORT

To reach the most popular Himalayan shrines and main link routes, the overnight Mussoorie Express train from Old Delhi for Dehra Dun has some carriages which go on to Kotdwar railhead. These carriages are uncoupled at Nazimabad at around 4.30am and connected to the Kotdwar shuttle service, a 45-minute journey. The Mussoorie Express passes through Hardwar at 6am which has a narrow gauge rail link to Rishikesh, 16km away. From Hardwar public buses and taxis are also available. (Private buses can be chartered through bus operators all over the Garhwal and Kumaon region.) Nazimabad, Hardwar and Dehra Dun are also connected by trains coming from Calcutta, Varanasi and Lucknow. The Inter State Bus Terminal (ISBT), Old Delhi, operates almost hourly services after 5am to Dehra Dun, Hardwar, Rishikesh and Kotdwar, which are the most convenient starting points for temple viewing and trekking tours to Garhwal.

Rishikesh to Gangotri Route

Place	Alt.	Distance	Remarks
Rishikesh	340m		Route up to Dharasu same as for Yamunotri
Dharasu	1036m	120km	
Uttarkashi	1158m	28km	Religious town
Maneri	1372m	10km	39m high Hydel Dam on the Bhagirathi
Lata	.....	15km	Route crosses the Ganges to Kush-kalyan and Kedarnath tracks
Bhatwari	1677m	19km	Trekking to Dayara meadows
Gangnani	1982m	14km	Hotwater springs
Sukhi	2744m	18km	
Harsil	2591m	13km	
Lanka	2652m	13km	Old route to Tibet, currently closed to all
Gangotri	3140m	10km	Trekking routes starting point

Uttarkashi: District headquarters bustling with activity on the right bank of the Bhagirathi. There are several temples in the town, the most important being Vishwanath. There is also a petrol station (petrol is not available beyond Uttarkashi). The state-run Nehru Institute of Mountaineering is also located here, about 6km across the river. Porters and provisions for trekking tours should be organised from Uttarkashi. You need to negotiate rates for porters and other service conditions with the porter agencies. Only part of the payment should be made in advance, the balance being paid on completion of the tour. Everything is available at the market for provisions - fresh vegetables, fruit, kerosene, etc. There is a tourist bungalow, some simple hotels, eating places, banks and hospital in the town. Foreign money can be exchanged in the bank but it is a very time-consuming and complicated affair! Buses are available for all destinations within Garhwal.

Harsil: The main village of Harsil is situated on the right bank of the Bhagirathi. Foreigners are not at present allowed to cross the river for security reasons. Henrich Harrer, author of *Seven Years in Tibet*, escaped from a prison in Dehra Dun to Tibet during the second world war via Harsil, Lanka and Nilang.

Lanka: At the confluence of the Jadganga and Bhagirathi rivers,

below Bhaironghati, is a spring whose waters taste like soda and
are believed to cure all stomach ailments.

The bridge over the Jadganga (Janvi) linking Lanka with
Bhaironghati is 103m high, one of the highest bridges in the world.
The Bhagirathi flows through a deep gorge between Gangotri and
Kopang near Harsil. Several feet of rock has been eroded over the
years by the river.

Rishikesh to Kedarnath Route

Place	Alt.	Distance	Remarks
Rishikesh	340m		
Deoprayag	472m	70km	Confluence of the Bhagirathi and Alaknanda
Srinagar	579m	35km	
Rudraprayag	610m	34km	Road branch to Badrinath via Karna-prayag. Confluence of the Alaknanda and Mandakini
Tilwara	671m	9km	Connected with Tehri via Ghansali
Agastmuni	762m	10km	
Kund	976m	15km	Road branch to Ukhimath for Chopta-Tungnath
Guptkashi	1479m	5km	Road branch to Kalimath, 13km, and trek to Madmaheshwar
Phata	1601m	14km	
Sonprayag	1829m	12km	
Gaurikund	1982m	5km	Bus terminal
Rambara	2591m	7km	On foot
Garurchatti	3262m	4km	On foot
Kedarnath	3581m	3km	On foot

Srinagar: Srinagar, founded in the 14th century, was the capital of
Garhwal till 1816. It is a busy town with a university and a
famous Kamaleshwar temple dedicated to Lord Shiva. Women
who do not have children pray at this temple along with their
husbands on the night of Baikunth Chaturdasi (a religious day)
in November. They remain standing throughout the night,
holding an oil lamp, whilst other members of the family sing
devotional songs to keep them awake. If a woman is too tired to
stand, her husband may take her place for a while, but the
religious fervour and wish to have a child is so great that the

woman mostly manages the prayer on her own. So many couples wish to attend this special prayer that an advance booking for space in the room is required.

Rishikesh to Yamunotri Route via Tehri

Place	Alt.	Distance	Remarks
Rishikesh	340m		
Narendranagar	1067m	16km	
Chamba	1534m	46km	The road from Mussoorie 55km away, also joins here. Mountain views
Tehri	770m	21km	Routes to Kedarnath and Badrinath via Ghansali and Srinagar. Site of Tehri Dam
Dharasu	1036m	37km	The road alongside the Bhagirathi goes to Uttarkashi
Rarikadanda	2280m	24km	
Barkot	1828m	31km	Shorter route from Dehra Dun/ Mussoorie, 128km away, joins here
Sayanachatti	1982m	29km	
Hanumanchatti	2134m	5km	Road ends here
Phoolchatti	2561m	5km	On foot
Jankibaichatti	2576m	2km	On foot
Yamunotri	3323m	6km	On foot

Dehra Dun to Yamunotri Route via Mussoorie

Place	Alt.	Distance	Remarks
Dehra Dun	701m		Another route via Dakpather, about 80km away
Mussoorie	1921m	33km	
Kempty falls	1524m	12km	
Yamuna bridge	772m	16km	Route from Dakpather joins here
Damta	1372m	25km	
Naugaon	1524m	28km	Change of route for Purola-Netwar
Barkot	1828m	11km	Road from Rishikesh joins here for Sayana chatti, Hanuman chatti, Phoolchatti etc.

Rishikesh to Badrinath Route

Place	Alt.	Distance	Remarks
Rishikesh	340m		
Rudraprayag	610m	139km	(Details given under Rishikesh-Kedarnath route)
Gauchar	790m	20km	
Karanprayag	795m	11km	Confluence of the Alaknanda and Pinder
Nandprayag	914m	22km	
Chamoli	1069m	10km	Road from Okhimath-Chopta joins here
Pipalkoti	1311m	17km	
Helong	1542m	17km	Start point for Kalpeshwar, 6km, one of the Panch Kedars
Joshimath	1890m	14km	Very important town (details in Hill Stations section)
Vishnuprayag	1372m	10km	
Govindghat	1829m	10km	Trek start for Valley of Flowers, 14km, to Ghangaria
Pandukeshwar	1835m	4km	
Hanuman chatti	2286m	9km	Start of 13km drive with several hairpin bends
Badrinath	3110m	15km	

Karanprayag: It is believed that Karan, of the *Mahabharata* epic, worshipped the sun here and was blessed with an impregnable body shield. It is a big busy market centre with a petrol pump, banks, a tourist bungalow, several eating places and some simple hotels. Roads go to Ranikhet, Almora, Tharali, and to the Rupkund trek.

Nandprayag: This little town is on the confluence of the Nandakini and Alaknanda rivers. From here the road branches to Ghat, 20km, and to the start point for the base camp of Mt. Trishul and Nandaghunti from the southern side, and the trekking route to Kwari pass via Ramani.

Pipalkoti: A big prosperous village with several shops, eating places, simple hotels and a petrol pump. 5km along the road from here is Garurganga. According to legend Garur, the carrier of Vishnu, lived here and the pebbles found in the Garurganga stream are blessed by the Garur with the power to ward off poisonous snake and insect bites.

Govindghat: This is the terminus for the Valley of Flowers, 14km, and the Hemkund shrine of Sikhs, 6km, from Ghangharia.

Hanuman chatti: The drive to Hanuman chatti is along the Alaknanda, which looks ferocious during monsoons. All vehicles stop here to take blessings at the temple of the monkey god, Hanuman, in which the temple priest places a red mark on your forehead. You would do well to put a few coins on the priest's plate for receiving the blessing!

Kedarnath to Badrinath

There are two routes to Badrinath from Kedarnath. The more conventional route is by a regular bus via Rudraprayag and Chamoli, 243km. (Details of this route from Rudraprayag onwards are given under the Rishikesh-Badrinath route.) The second route is shorter by 13km and goes from Kund to Chopta-Man-dal-Gopeshwar and joins the Rishikesh-Badrinath route at Chamoli. This is a very pretty route if you have your own transport and are self-supported as there are only a few shops on the way and a regular supply of essential provisions is unreliable. The drive right up to Gopeshwar is through beautiful valleys and forests with Himalayan views. This area has been designated the Kedarnath Wildlife Sanctuary. About 6km from Ukhimath at Mastura is a 6km footpath to the beautiful Deoraia tal lake at about 2600m. It would be worthwhile to spend a day here by the lake to watch the sun rise and set on the Chaukhamba range. The road winds through thick deodar (cedar) and oak forest to Dogalbita with a rest house above the road. A short break here and a hot cup of tea in a tea house is recommended, where you can enjoy the surrounding vibrant green foliage and splendid view of the Himalaya. Chopta is only 15 minutes' drive from here at 2600m. There are a few tea houses in shacks and a tourist bungalow. Chopta is thickly wooded, interspersed with patches of meadow. Here you can sit for hours grazing at the magnificent ranges of Mt. Kedarnath, Chaukhamba and Nilkanth, forming a wide arch. It is a nice place for camping. From here, Tungnath at 3700m is only 3km away and provides still better views of the peaks, including Mt. Nandadevi. It is a lovely spot to spend a day or two. Descending back to Chopta and about 9km further along the road is the state-run Musk deer breeding centre. At present there are 16 male and female Musk deer in this centre, which can be seen with permission from the warden. Mandal is a 28km drive through dense forest but only 12km if you decide to walk down via a footpath.

The route beyond Mandal is through villages famous for growing oranges. 9km from Mandal is the start of a 17km footpath at the village of Gangolgaon for Rudranath temple. 3km further on is Gopeshwar, the district headquarters of Chamoli, with a big market place, hospital, banks, a petrol pump, tourist bungalow and simple hotels.

The next main town on this route is Chamoli, 10km along on the bank of the Alaknanda, where the main road to Badrinath from Rishikesh and Kedarnath joins.

Haldwani/Kathgodam to Nainital Route

Place	Alt.	Distance	Remarks
Haldwani			
Kathgodam		5km	
Jeolikot		18km	Road branch to Almora and Ranikhet
Nainital	1938m	17km	

Kathgodam-Almora-Gwaldom Route

Place	Alt.	Distance	Remarks
Kathgodam	300m		
Jeolikot		18km	Road branch to Nainital
Bhowali	1706m	13km	
Khairna	1250m	32km	Road branch to Ranikhet, 20km
Almora	1645m	35km	
Kosi		13km	
Someshwar		27km	Road branch to Bageshwar
Kausani		12km	
Baijnath	1125m	19km	
Gwaldom		21km	

Tanakput to Pithoragarh Route

Place	Alt.	Distance	Remarks
Tanakpur			
Champawat	1615m	61km	Scenic place with many temples
Lohaghat	1750m	13km	Beautiful town with tall cedar trees
Ghat		43km	Change of route for Gangolighat and Chaukori, 67km from Pithoragarh
Pithoragarh	1650m	20km	

Pithoragarh to Munsyari Route

Place	Alt.	Distance	Remarks
Pithoragarh	1650m		
Jauljibi		68km	Change of route for Thal and Chaukori
Baram	1150m	15km	
Madkot	1300m	30km	
Munsyari	2290m	22km	

Karanprayag to Munsyari Route

Place	Alt.	Distance	Remarks
Karanprayag	795m		
Simli		7km	Road branch to Ranikhet, 110km, via Gairsain and Dwarahat
Tharali		35km	Change of route for Deval, 13km
Gwaldom		21km	
Baijnath		21km	Change of route for Almora, 71km
Bageshwar		19km	
Chaukori	2020m	45km	
Thal		17km	Another route to Munsyari via Didihat, Jauljibi and Baram, 118km
Tejam		10km	
Munsyari	2290m	50km	

PART III
Trekking in General

"I still believe that Garhwal is the most beautiful
country of all high Asia. Neither the primitive
immensity of Karakoram, the aloof domination of
Mt. Everest, the softer Caucasian beauties of the
Hindu Kush, nor any of the many other regions of
Himalaya can compare with Garhwal. Mountain
and valley, forest and alp, birds and animals,
butterflies and flowers all combine to make a sum of
delight unsurpassed elsewhere."

(T.G. Longstaff, *The Ascent of Nandadevi*)

Longstaff's well-known quote sums up perfectly the natural
attractions of Uttarakhand, and although much has changed in the
area since 1937 the beauty which so enchanted the early mountaineers
is still there for the present-day trekker to discover and enjoy. The
flower studded meadows still make perfect camping sites, wildlife
still inhabits the forests, and the great peaks and glittering panoramas
are, of course, unchanged. Some of the trekking routes described are
the very same ones used by those early explorers. Other routes are
ancient cross-country pilgrimage trails now replaced by roads, or
lead to glaciers and mountain lakes. A few cross high passes, others
remain at moderate altitudes, and they range from day treks along
busy paths to trips lasting weeks and requiring expedition-style
self-sufficiency. Some treks, such as the Source of the Ganges or the
Valley of Flowers, are names known to trekkers, but the majority of
routes remain known to relatively few at present. The peaks of the
Uttarakhand are not as well known as the Nepalese giants, but
bigger is not necessarily better, and although Everest may glory in
its "aloof domination" it cannot compare in beauty with Shivling,
Neelkanth, Nandadevi or many of the other peaks of the Garhwal.
Unfortunately, the sanctuary around the best known peak,
Nandadevi, is closed, but there are plenty of opportunities for

Breakfast at Shivling

Mt Trishul (Photo: John Martin)
On the trail, Panchuli range in background (Photo: Author)

Mt Hathi and Gori Parbat (Photo: John Martin)
Nanda Devi (Photo: John Martin)

spectacular views of the 'Mountain Goddess'. In fact it is a feature of all the treks that there are continuously changing views of a magnificent array of summits. The combination of natural beauty and cultural interest make trekking in Garhwal and Kumaon uniquely rewarding. Unless you go as part of an organised tour it is best suited to experienced travellers and trekkers, who can cope with the lack of facilities, the unavailability of western food (or anything but the basic Indian diet), and the problems of inaccurate maps and unreliable porters, among many others. Anyone arriving after trekking in Nepal and expecting to easily hire guides and porters and find lodges with hot showers and cold cokes is in for a shock. On most treks in Uttarakhand a different, more self-reliant, approach to trekking is required. The trekker requires a spirit of adventure and a sense of humour, because there will certainly be times when if they don't laugh, they will cry. It is one of the great attractions of the area that it is 'unspoilt' and 'uncommercialised', and this makes trekking there both more difficult and more rewarding. The journeys which are really memorable are usually those where success has come only after an effort, bringing a sense of achievement to the final arrival at your goal. All trekking is like this but in Uttarakhand both the effort and the final reward are that bit greater. If you go trekking with a little experience and the right attitude you will come away astonished at the beauty and grandeur of the scenery, with a richer understanding of one of the world's great religions, and almost certainly with a powerful desire to return.

ORGANISED TREKS

These are the easiest way to undertake a trek but require some compromises. Fifteen years ago none of the companies selling trekking tours in the Himalaya were operating in the area, but the situation has improved and it is now possible to go to a specialist travel agent at home, particularly in the UK, and book a trek in Uttarakhand. Obviously you will be restricted to what is on offer in the brochure and the price will be higher, but you should get what you pay for in terms of services and organisation. Trips of around 3 weeks are the norm, and you can expect everything to be taken care of for you, leaving you free to enjoy the trek. You should be met at the airport, have your accommodation and train tickets reserved and a private coach. On trek food will be provided by accompanying cooks, tents and your baggage carried by porters, and a knowledgeable guide will accompany you on a programme designed to make the most of a short visit, but without the trekking being too arduous. The choice of tour leader is critical and since contact with local people is one of the most rewarding features of this type of holiday, an experienced local guide is best. None can introduce you to a country as well as a native. When not camping, accommodation used on the tour may be a bit primitive, and the diet is likely to be more Indian than western, both because western food is not available, and the available cooks are not trained to provide pizza and steak. The standard of service in Nepal has been built up over many years, but Uttarakhand is at the beginning of that process. You will still have a good time, but things will just be a little rougher round the edges.

The important thing to recognise about such a holiday is that joining a group requires some compromise. You will be on a fixed itinerary, and cannot go further should you feel like it, or stay longer at any one place. Your menus too will be fixed, as will meal times and the daily routine of the group, and you should respect the advice of the leader, even if you are inclined to disagree with it. Your companions could be of any age, sex or nationality and be novice or experienced trekkers, so everyone will have to make the effort to get along. With that little bit of give and take strangers usually become friends and the tour is a success. On one occasion two members of a German group I was leading to Rupkund were impatient with the pace and wanted to go further each day. They finally insisted so vehemently that, against my advice and only because the other group members were prepared to go along with them, they got their way. That night some group members showed mild signs of altitude sickness as a result of climbing too fast, all were very tired, and because the cook and the porter carrying the food could not keep up, the meal was very late. The extra distance was hard for the porters. It took a lot of persuasion to stop them from deserting us there and then. As it was, the group had to pay a large bonus to get them to finish the tour. Next day the two who had insisted on the harder pace were exhausted and unfit to go on, and also because of the condition of the rest of the group we turned back without completing the tour. With a steady pace and time for acclimatisation everyone would have reached Rupkund and enjoyed themselves. The two who caused all the trouble were experienced trekkers and thought they knew better, but they should have realised the guide is there because he knows best.

Using A Local Agent

A second approach is to bypass a travel agent at home and work directly with a trekking agent in India or Uttarakhand who can advise, help you choose your trek and make all your arrangements for you (a procedure that is so complex it cannot effectively be done from abroad). You will then have the confidence which comes from expert advice and the reassurance of knowing porters will be reliable. More importantly you will not be restricted by what is on offer in a brochure, but can arrange a tailor-made tour of your own. At present your options are limited by the small number of reputable agencies based in Garhwal with local knowledge and experience in organising tours for western visitors.

GOING IT ALONE

Once you decide to do without an agent you are committed to arriving and undertaking your trek without any advance arrangements, since any procedures for booking staff or transport are so complicated they can only be effectively undertaken by someone on the spot. This means you will have to allow time for using public transport, searching out porters and finding accommodation, and should any of these not be available, be adaptable enough to change your plans. It is best not to set off with rigid plans, intending to reach a fixed point each day, but to allow a few days' leeway in your programme in case of unexpected holdups. Trying to accomplish a trek on a tight schedule can only lead to frustration, and those who set off with a flexible, easy-going approach will enjoy themselves more. In India even simple tasks like getting a seat on a bus can be difficult, and organisation and efficiency are not a strong point of many of the agencies independent trekkers are likely to deal with. You will need patience and perseverance. Despite the hassles that may be involved, going it alone is still one of the most satisfying ways of trekking and is obviously the cheapest way for those on a tight budget. If you go in the right frame of mind, and can take the difficulties in your stride, you will have a closer relationship with both locals and pilgrims, maybe some unexpected companions, and the freedom to stop or move on as the mood takes you. One important decision you will have to make is whether to hire porters for your trek. The advantages of doing without porters are complete independence, and avoiding all the difficulties employing them tends to bring, while the disadvantage is having to carry everything yourself. Labouring under a huge backpack certainly takes some of the enjoyment out of trekking, but with modern equipment, and provided you are prepared to live off simple rations, it is possible to trek without porters and without too large a pack. The ability to get along with your trekking companions is essential, especially in stressful situations, and you should discuss thoroughly what you each expect from the trip, or want to achieve - arguing about what to do next once you are on trek is not a good idea. Apart from companionship having several in the group shares the load and is safer. Should you decide to trek alone you will find the area safe, provided you use your common sense. Women travelling alone should take particular care about their dress, noting that the local women's costume covers them from neck to ankles - shorts or tight T-shirts should be avoided; long skirts and loose blouses or shirts are recommended.

Trekking With Guides And Porters
Using either guides or porters is a difficult business and can create more problems than it solves. Apart from seasonal work on the trails there is little regular work in portering, and what porters there are, are not used to working for trekkers. You are also unlikely to find anyone with experience as a guide since there have never been enough visitors to establish a trained and experienced corps of guides. Trekkers must therefore employ local villagers, who are free from other tasks, and this means there is no guarantee of availability or reliability. In some of the major stopover towns on the pilgrimage routes, such as Uttarkashi, Joshimath or Munsyari, you will find porter agencies and there are always likely to be porters

around, but they may only be used to working locally or on particular trails. Nevertheless, it may be possible to employ someone for your trek here, when no one is available at your starting point or further along the road. It is worth breaking your journey to check things out. Ask in the villages at the start of your trek, hoping someone is free and willing to accompany you, but this may take some time, and you will be in a poor bargaining position. In Uttarkashi district the District Board approved porter agencies are notorious for providing troublemaker porters and for demanding 25 to 35 per cent commission on daily wages, even from porters not provided by them or porters provided by other approved agencies.

Negotiating with porters is difficult and is made doubly so by language problems. It is important to try and sort out the details or you will have problems later on. The government prescribed load for porters is 25kg, on top of which they carry their own goods and provisions, and wages are negotiable, depending on how good you are at haggling, the length and difficulty of the trek, and how desperate the porter thinks you are! You will be expected to pay for the days of their return journey, and they may insist on very short stages, as little as 5/6km at times. For this reason it is often best to agree in advance the number of days for the trek, and the stages in which it is to be covered. A tip is also expected at the end of the trip and if you intend to climb high or into snow conditions you must be sure that porters are suitably equipped. Even when you think everything is agreed and are underway new demands can be made, but it is often the case that the greater the number of porters, the more likely you are to have trouble with them. If you just hire one or two men and can come to an amicable agreement, you will probably get on fine, and find they act as guide and porters combined.

There is no doubt a good porter is an ideal helper and companion. The distinction between a guide and a porter is open to interpretation. Anyone who knows the way can be a guide, but the author has experience of local men putting themselves forward, when in fact they didn't know the way. Sometimes a man capable of arranging a few porters offers his services as a guide so that he does not have to carry any load and also demands higher wages. The majority of the trails in the Uttarakhand are clear and well marked. Most of the routes described here can be followed without the additional aid of a guide. Where any route is particularly difficult, and I have advised finding a guide, this can usually be done in villages on the approach to the difficult section, so the guide is not needed for the whole trek.

In some places, and for certain routes, it may be possible to hire mules to carry baggage. One man may have up to two mules, and he would travel with you to look after them. Each mule should carry 70/80kg, but again you will have to negotiate, and the mules will cover roughly the same daily stages as porters. Porters will use either a wicker basket held by a head strap or tie up the load before strapping it on their backs, while mules need loads which are balanced and of a uniform shape. In either case the straps and frames of rucksacks are awkward and simple canvas holdalls are the best idea. They should be tough enough to withstand knocks and bangs and lockable. Very strong plastic bags are also useful as waterproof liners and you should pack carefully, ensuring you have everything you need for the day in your own small pack as it is difficult to gain access to the loads once they are tied up.

Two examples showing the experiences of my friend Robert Howard will illustrate the pros and cons of hiring porters. "At the village of Wan I found a man to accompany me to Rupkund. He coped with my very heavy sack easily, and when we were struck by a storm which was so cold I lost all feeling in my hands, he quickly lit a charcoal fire inside the hollow of a burnt-out tree. Higher up he breasted a way through deep snow, and led the way unerringly though all the paths were buried. He was in every way a capable guide-cum-porter and a good companion. A second porter/guide hired at the largest agency in Uttarkashi proved a liability. He could carry little, and not knowing the way led us into difficulty. His camp craft was such that I had to light the fires and taught him how to make chapattis, and eventually he ran off, though by that time I was glad to be rid of him."

WHEN TO GO
The trekking season in Garhwal is determined by winter snowfall and the monsoon. The following general information gives a clear picture of the weather pattern and its effects on the trekker.

January/February
Winter. Freezing temperatures and heavy snows close down the

higher valleys. Clouds restrict the views. Snows may fall as low as 1400m.

March

Winter. Snow may continue in the high regions, but treks up to about 3000m are possible. Rhododendrons bloom profusely. Snow views are very clear and close.

April

Pre-monsoon season. Treks up to about 3500m are possible depending on snow conditions. Spring growth at lower altitudes is abundant, the wheat harvest starts at the end of the month and rhododendrons are in full bloom. This is the second-driest month behind October/November with clear views. In the higher valleys and pastures snow may still be accumulating.

May

This is a month of rapid thaws, and while the pastures and passes above 3500m may still be snow covered in early May, they will be clear by the end of the month and carpeted with early spring flowers. Localised thunderstorms are common and though unlikely to last more than an hour they can be severe, with thunder, lightning and hail. The lower hills and valleys start to feel uncomfortably hot with the gradual rise in temperature. Views are usually good. This is one of the best trekking months.

June

Monsoon. The rains do not normally break until the second week, but the period is very hot and humid in the lower hills and valleys. Thunderstorms remain frequent too. This is also one of the peak times for pilgrimage, putting the maximum strain on all services. When the monsoon breaks it can cause chaos by washing down landslides of loose rocks and dry soil, which block the roads. With the thaw continuing trekking routes above 4000m are open.

July & August

Monsoon. These are the monsoon months, when trekking is at its most difficult. Paths and roads are affected by landslides, and the clouds only lift occasionally so views are poor. It will rain almost every day, sometimes nearly non-stop for 2-3 days. The almost every day, sometimes nearly non-stop for 2-3 days. The wet weather also brings out the leeches in a few regions. However, this is by far the best season for flowers, which proliferate in the upper valleys, creating a carpet of brilliantly mixed colours. Although it is wet, it remains warm and the transport problems are not insuperable. If possible one should opt for organised treks during monsoons.

September

Post-monsoon season. The rains stop in mid September. It may, however, take a while before all the road repairs are complete. The temperature is still pleasant, and the air fresh and clear after monsoon. Towards the middle of the month, and into October, the majority of trekking routes are open.

October

Post-monsoon season. This is an ideal month for trekking. There are magnificent views and a lot of sunshine. Temperatures in the lower valleys will be more comfortable and higher up it will be cold, but not bitterly so. Above 3500m snow may fall occasionally.

This is also the peak harvest season, when the fields are full of villagers harvesting the rice paddy, lentils, millet and vegetables to stock up for the long winter ahead. This may make finding porters more difficult.

November

Post-monsoon season. Another good time for trekking, and traditionally the driest month, during which the harvest is completed. The temperature will be dropping fast and any bad weather may bring snow, even as low as 2000m.

December

Winter. Though the start of the month may provide some clear days suitable for trekking, there is always a threat of heavy snow and the temperature will be uncomfortably cold. After mid December treks above 3000m are not recommended.

WHAT TO TAKE

This will largely be a matter of personal choice, but the best advice is to take as little as possible, within reason of course. Whether you are carrying everything yourself, or intending to use porters, there is no point in carrying excess weight, yet many people do. It would be foolish to go under-equipped, but when setting out for a strange place it is hard to know what you will need. If the destination is also an environment which can be hazardous the natural inclination is to go prepared for every eventuality. The only eventuality you can't cope with is that your pack is too heavy to carry! Trekkers who are going with an organised tour, or have booked porters through a local agent, may not think the weight issue is so critical, but it is still important. Many companies will set a weight limit which may be as little as 12kg to ensure porters are not overloaded and keep porterage costs down. Those who ignore this often have to wait until last for the porter with their bag to stagger in to camp, and feel terribly guilty at the sight of the wearisome burden which is their kitbag. If you are going to use porters remember to take kitbags, rather than rucksacks, and practise packing them into sensible porter loads before you leave. A porter should be able to carry two 10kg bags tied together plus a tent. Modern equipment with a weight-conscious design can be expensive and you may have to decide whether it is worth buying a new tent which is half the weight of your old one. Buy the best you can afford, as the demands of Himalayan trekking will quickly find the faults in cheap equipment.

Footwear
Getting this right is vital. Hopefully anyone going on a trek is an experienced walker who knows what type of footwear suits them best and it is always a good idea to stick with what you know. Modern running shoes, which are built to high cushioning and stability design specifications, are perfectly adequate for trekking below the snowline, or even for the occasional crossing of a snowy path. Their grip is not a match for mountain boots in slippery conditions, but many companies now produce trainers intended for trails or mountain running with studded or waffle soles. One thing trainers do not give is ankle support so they are not suitable for very rough terrain, nor can they be waterproofed. Lightweight boots in all sorts of specifications are now readily available, made from a variety of materials. These are much easier to break in than the heavier mountain boots with a steel shank and do offer ankle support, though they are not as easily waterproofed as leather boots, or as strong. Many also have Vibram soles and are ideal

trekking boots. Trekking is very hard on footwear and strength is an important quality; so too are stability and grip. Leather can also be effectively waterproofed and, if you are doing any very high level trekking, crampons can be fitted. It is also easier to fit gaiters when crossing snow.

Whatever you choose to wear make sure the shoes are well broken in before you set off. Starting the first day of your trek with new boots is asking for trouble. It is also a good idea to put in a shock-absorbing inner sole, such as Sorbothane, and carry spare laces and a small tube of suitable glue in case the sole comes unstuck. If this is also suitable for tent repairing, all the better. Most trekkers will want something to change into at the campsite, and simple sandals or canvas pumps are ideal, and can be worn for river crossings too. Experienced walkers will have their own ideas on the best socks, but the most favoured combination seems to be thin undersock of synthetic material, which should be changed and washed regularly, and a second outer pair of woollen socks.

Tents And Sleeping Bags

It is wise to take a tent as you then have the flexibility of choosing where to stop, and the certainty of secure accommodation if you fail to complete a daily stage as expected. A tent also gives you the choice of privacy and the freedom to stay as long as you wish on some of the world's most magnificent camping grounds. The 'bugyals' of the Uttarakhand are campsites as near to perfection as any trekker can imagine. Flower-strewn meadows with springs of clear water, surrounded by forest rich in wildlife, and studded with lakes, would delight anyone. However, add to that a panorama of Himalayan peaks stretching across the horizon and sharply defined in the crystal clear air, and you have more than enough reason to take your tent.

Most tents have waterproofed nylon outer from which an inner tent is suspended. Cotton inners are a little heavier, but attract less condensation than those made of nylon. Dome tents give you considerable head room, as do those using a transverse hoop, or you can choose tunnel tents, or wedge-shaped tents with one lower end where you put your feet. A bell-end where you can store your pack, repack when it's raining outside or, with care, cook in foul weather is very useful, as is a snow valence. Spare pegs and a spare pole should also be carried. Even if they offer, do not let local staff put up your tent, as they do not have the necessary experience - it will be wrongly stressed and zips and guys could get broken.

To keep you comfortable inside your tent, a good sleeping bag is an essential item, and for most treks you need a 3 season bag, which will keep you warm down to freezing point. If you don't feel the cold a 2 season bag may suffice for treks below 3000m, provided you use a good insulation mat. For warmth, down sleeping bags are probably best, and they compress well too, but they are hard to dry out or wash, and useless when wet. Most bags will therefore have synthetic filling. If you have a zip you can at least adjust the temperature, or open a bag out to serve as a quilt. Closed cell foam pads are very popular for mattresses and are light to carry, so buy the best you can afford. Air mattresses are not very practical on trek, but the self-inflating Thermarest products are purpose designed to withstand the hardships of outdoor life. Extra clothing can make a good pillow, but some prefer to take an inflatable pillow with them.

Other Equipment
If you are carrying a load yourself the other major item of equipment is a rucksack. Most models today have internal frames and ergonomic designs, which means fitting to the body for maximum carrying efficiency. You should remember that no rucksack is waterproof and use internal plastic liners. A zipped lower compartment is useful for carrying a sleeping bag, or putting a damp tent in, and side pockets are invaluable for things you might need at short notice. They can also be used for fuel containers which you want to keep separate from the main load. Sometimes pouches for cameras (or anything else) can be fitted onto the hip belts for easy access, and if you carry an iceaxe or crampons you will need the appropriate straps to attach these. Generally speaking you should pack heavier items near the top to avoid making your centre of gravity too low. Using a variety of internal stuff-sacks helps to separate your belongings, and gives you somewhere to put the smelly washing!

For trekking in groups and with porters you will need a simple day pack big enough to carry warm clothing, waterproofs, camera, waterbottle, and your diary or reading books. You will almost inevitably be passing through one of the bigger towns like Dehra Dun before you start trekking, and if you are returning the same way it is worthwhile taking a lockable holdall which you can leave in storage at your hotel or with your agent. Into this you can put spare clothes and footwear for your return, and anything else you might not need on trek. A waterbottle is essential and it is advisable to always keep it full. You need at least a litre capacity and a secure top to stop any leakage. For small groups a collapsible water carrier might be useful when you are camped some distance away from the water source, and a small plastic bottle to carry in your hand and drink from while you are walking. You will need a torch and sufficient batteries to last your trip - long-life alkaline batteries are the best. A head torch is the most useful kind, and some will take long-life, or extra powerful, bulbs. Be sure you have a spare. It is often too hot to wear waterproofs when it rains, so some trekkers like to carry an umbrella. Others carry a walking stick, which is specially useful when walking with heavy loads, and for crossing rivers, or fending off dogs. A pocket knife, including a tin opener, scissors and tweezers is useful, and a small sewing kit may be needed for repairs. Earplugs can ensure your peace in noisy accommodation. Given the maps available, a compass is not really necessary, though it might help you identify the peaks around you. Some people like to carry altimeters and thermometers. The former are often dependent on air pressure. Simple and safe thermometers are readily available. A small pair of binoculars can greatly enhance your appreciation of the wildlife, and especially the birdlife, around you. All you really need for washing yourself, your hair and your clothes is a bar of soap, and this is readily available almost everywhere. A face flannel can be useful, and some carry a piece of string for a clothes line and a few miniature pegs, though washing one or two items a day and walking with them tied to your rucksack works just as well. Toilet paper is only available in the larger towns.

If you are going to spend any time in snow or on glaciers you might need gaiters, possibly even an iceaxe and crampons, though they are not required for the treks described in this book, unless you go out of season. For extended periods on snow take proper goggles, which offer protection all around the eye, glacier cream and lip salve. For lower treks take sunglasses and suncream, and remember a hat can stop you from getting a headache in the sun. Attaching a flap can also save you from painfully sunburned ears and neck. You will need a money belt or pouch for your passport and money. For your entertainment you might like to take dice or playing cards, and most people carry a book or two. Pictures of your family are handy to show to those you meet. A personal stereo and some tapes can also be carried, and with a record-and-play facility you can have endless fun with the local children. A simple Hindi phrase book will help you get to grips with the language, and many people like to write a diary when travelling. If you want to take anything to give to the children biros for their school work are best.

Passport And Money
You should carry your passport with you at all times. Police or military officials might ask to see it, and if you do not have it available, there will be considerable problems. You will need it for registering at hotels and tourist lodges. Rural India suffers from a chronic shortage of small change, so you should not go trekking with too many large notes. Change all the money you need for the trek before leaving for the hills, taking as many small notes and coins as possible. Dirty and torn notes will not be taken in the hills, though there is no problem with holed notes.

Equipment Checklist
The following is intended not as a master list from which everything should be taken, but as a checklist from which you can select what to take, and to help ensure nothing important is left behind. No quantities are given as these will depend on the duration of the trek, but provided you wash clothes regularly you need take no more than 3 of any item.

Passport and money
Maps and guidebook
Tent, spares and repair kit, or
    bivouac sack
Rucksack or day pack
Holdall to leave at hotel and
    kitbags for porters
Plastic liners, sheeting and
    compression straps
Polythene bags and stuff sacks
Money belt or pouch
Sleeping bag and insulation mat
Boots or trainers, spare laces,
Waterproofing, repair glue
Camp shoes and socks
Trousers or breeches (men)

Shorts (men)
Skirt or culottes (women)
Thermal underwear, tops and
    bottoms
Mittens and gloves
Shirts or blouses
Underwear
Sweater and jacket
Hats and/or balaclava
Wind and waterproof outer
shell, tops and bottoms
Scarf and handkerchiefs
Bathing costume
Sunglasses, suncream, glacier
    cream and lip salve
Waterbottles and carriers
Water purifiers, first aid kit and
    sewing kit
Torch, spare bulbs and batteries
Washing kit and towel

Toilet paper and shaving kit
Feminine hygiene materials
Camera, accessories and film
Diary and writing materials
Pocket knife
Matches or lighter
Candles or nitelights
Cooking stove, spares and
cleaning materials
Fuel and fuel containers, fuel
    filter and stove windshield
Food supplies
Cooking pots and pans, mug,
cutlery
Scourer cloth, polythene bags
    and plastic pots for food
    containers
Gaiters, goggles, iceaxe and
    crampons

The following are optional items:
Walking stick and umbrella (can
be acquired locally)
Books, stereo and tapes
Clothes line and pegs

Playing cards or dice
Pens for give-aways
Altimeter, thermometer,
compass, binoculars

HEALTH AND FITNESS

If you do not already do so as a regular part of your daily routine you should certainly start some sort of fitness programme several months in advance of departure. Hopefully you will already be a regular hiker or mountain walker.

There is no point in thinking you will get fitter as the trek progresses - you will just be tired, and suffer unnecessary aches and pains, which will take the enjoyment out of your holiday. The Himalaya are on a scale which it is hard to imagine, even for regular hillwalkers, and it is unwise to wait until you arrive to find you are not fit enough to cope.

Running, with the emphasis on endurance, not speed, and without straining yourself to the point which actually causes injury, is the best form of exercise. Long walks on hilly terrain are obviously ideal, and cycling or cross-country skiing are good too. You should start off easily and aim to gradually build up the workload through regular exercise. Suddenly doing too much will be harmful.

If you intend to carry your own pack a few practice backpacking trips are needed. You might also stop using the car for short journeys.

Vaccinations

These should be planned well in advance with your own doctor, since some courses begin 4-6 weeks before departure, and you may have to schedule numerous injections. You certainly wouldn't want to have them all at once!

Tetanus   This should be up to date and a booster may be required.
Polio   Check a booster is not needed.
Typhoid   This is valid for 3 years. Further protection is given by booster shots.
Cholera   Some doctors regard it as ineffective and do not advise it. There has not been any known cholera epidemic in Garhwal and Kumaon for over three decades.

Yellow Fever injection is not required, but if you are arriving from an infected area you will need the internationally approved certificate to prove you have had the vaccination.

Rabies is present in both dogs and monkeys, and there is now a vaccine available which delays the onset of symptoms until further anti-rabies serum can be administered. Since the chances of being bitten are slim, it is probably best to rely on common sense when trekking. Avoid dogs, especially bitches with pups.

Malaria prophylaxis is recommended, though the disease is now being controlled in the plains and valleys, and is not likely to be a problem higher up. Your doctor will advise on the currently recommended dosage.

Consulting Your Doctor And Dentist

Consult your doctor regarding vaccinations and to check your heart, lungs and blood pressure. A dental checkup before departure will ensure any developing problems are dealt with - painful dental problems are the last thing you want to put up with on trek. If you do get toothache oil of cloves or the use of codeine will offer relief, while infections, such as abscesses, can be treated with antibiotics.

Hygiene

Common sense, rather than drugs, is your best protection against illness and careful attention to hygiene is vital.

- Always wash your hands thoroughly after going to the toilet and if necessary take your waterbottle to do so.
- Always wash your hands before eating. Hotels or lodges will have a jug of water handy for washing.
- Keep your fingernails short and clean.
- Purify all drinking water carefully and clean your teeth with purified water.

Water Purification

All water you drink must be thoroughly treated, and this includes water coming from household or hotel filters, and water you are not 100 per cent certain has been boiled. The only exception is at altitudes above all habitation and away from animal pastures. The best treatment is to use iodine. Keep a 2 per cent solution in a plastic dropper bottle and add 8 drops per litre, stir and then wait 20 minutes before drinking. If the water is cloudy, or from a suspect source, use a double strength, and if it is cold let it stand for longer, perhaps as much as an hour. This method is cheap and simple, and a small bottle will easily suffice for a whole trek. You will quickly get used to the taste, and after a while will not even notice it.

Devices which pump the water through extra-fine filters are also available and said to be very effective. The bottled water available in roadside shops is safe, and on long hot bus journeys a bottle of clean water from the fridge is a worthwhile purchase. Beware of milk made up from powder with unsterilised water, and if in doubt drink black tea. Tea is boiled up in a kettle with the milk. Don't drink anything with ice cubes, or eat ice cream.

Diarrhoea

This is a particular concern to trekkers as it can be a common and incapacitating illness, but with care and attention outbreaks can be limited. Do not eat unpeeled fruit, or uncooked foods such as salads, and avoid foods sold at the roadside which are left in the open and covered in flies. If possible, avoid fried food and meat.

Diarrhoea may be the result of a change of diet, or exertion in the sun and if it is not accompanied by cramps or vomiting, it is best to try simple remedies and not reach for expensive drugs straight away. Some people recommend a 24 hour fast, but this is not practical when trekking, so just eat lightly, using plain rice as the basis of your diet, and avoid fatty foods. Drink plenty to replace lost fluids, or take specially prepared rehydration drinks. Most simple outbreaks of diarrhoea are self-limiting and you should recover in a day or two.

If the attacks are a major inconvenience you can use anti-motility drugs such as Immodium or Lomotil. If your stools are very loose and frequent some doctors recommend 2 Lomotil at first, and one further tablet with each attack, until the diarrhoea stops.

If you are feeling feverish, and passing blood or mucous in your stools, you most likely have some type of dysentery and will need to rest and take antibiotic treatment. Self-treatment, without specific medical diagnosis, would not normally be recommended, though it may be needed if you are far from medical help.

Consult your doctor on which broad spectrum antibiotic to take with you, and watch out for any allergic reactions, in which case discontinue. Know what the correct dosage is, and be sure to complete the full course. You can take Lomotil at the same time to control the incidence of the diarrhoea.

Amoebic dysentery seems particularly common, and you may also encounter Giardia Lamblia, which can be virulent and very unpleasant. It is often accompanied by cramps and nausea, and particularly by wind with a distinctive sulphurous smell. If you are getting burps that taste like rotten eggs, plus the other symptoms, you may have Giardia, and the best treatment is a single 2 gram dose of Tinidazole. This is kept in most Indian pharmacies under the name Tiniba.

Local doctors and hospitals are very experienced in dealing with these illnesses, far more so than your doctor at home will be, and you should consult them if problems persist. The necessary drugs for treatment are also widely available over the counter and without prescription.

Altitude Sickness
This is a general term applied to several medical conditions brought on by the body's maladaption to the reduced oxygen content and air pressure at high altitudes. Nobody should be put off trekking for fear of suffering altitude sickness.

The best way to avoid altitude illness is a general rate of ascent, which allows the body to acclimatise properly. There can be no fixed rules as to what is a safe rate of ascent, as this will vary considerably from one individual to the next. The best acclimatisation is achieved through climbing high and sleeping low. It is the young and fit who may be most at risk, because feeling fit and full of youthful energy they are easily tempted to climb too high, too quickly. It is vital to take the right mental approach to altitude.

When you are walking keep a steady pace rather than rushing, take plenty of rests, and don't overexert yourself by carrying a heavy load. Overdoing things can also contribute to altitude sickness. It is natural to find breathing harder at altitude, and if you are struggling just take a short rest and you will feel better.

There is a drug called Diamox (Acetazolamide) to help avoid altitude sickness, but current advice is to try and acclimatise naturally, and only to use this drug if symptoms do appear, in which case it may aid acclimatisation. The dose is one 250mg tablet, twice a day. There is also a brand called Sustets, where you take one tablet at night. You must, however, consult your doctor for any side effects.

Above 3000m many people will experience some of the mild symptoms of altitude sickness. These are:

- Headache
- Loss of appetite
- Shortness of breath
- Sleeplessness or irregular breathing at night
- Mild nausea
- Feeling weak or light headed
- Slight swelling around the hands and face

They also vary in intensity, and in the elevations at which they appear. Provided any of the above symptoms remain mild it is usually safe to continue climbing slowly, but if the symptoms persist and start to get worse, descend and rest until you feel better.

If you are having difficulty in sleeping it is not a good idea to take sleeping pills, but you can treat headaches symptomatically.

Symptoms for severe altitude sickness are:

- Severe and persistent headache
- A noticeable loss of coordination
- Difficulty in breathing, even at rest
- Acute nausea and regular vomiting
- Extreme lassitude (disinterest in food, caring for yourself and acting in a withdrawn and anti-social way)
- Slurred speech and abnormal behaviour leading to confusion, delirium and coma
- Bubbling breath
- Severe coughing spasms, bringing up watery or pinkish sputum
- A very low daily urine output
- Rapid heart rate when resting
- Blueness of the face and lips

If any of these symptoms develop the trekker should descend straight away, preferably on the back of a porter or animal, and certainly not alone. The descent should continue beyond the point where relief occurs, where rest will lead to recovery.

Other Medical Problems

Sore feet are the medical problem you are most likely to get. Feet that are used to walking, and in well fitting boots and comfortable socks are less likely to suffer, but if you do get hot spots treat them by covering with plaster and padding, or moleskin, before blisters develop. Using Vaseline may prevent rubbing and tightening bootlaces before a descent can help prevent toe blisters. If blisters do develop you can either leave them, or burst them with a sterile needle, then cover with a dressing. There are many special blister treatment packs available now.

Sore throats are common in the dry air at high altitudes, so you might wish to take along some lozenges. For cold you can take a decongestant, or use codeine. Some antibiotic eye drops in case of eye infections are worth carrying, but avoid those containing penicillin. Any small wounds or cuts should be well cleaned and antiseptic cream applied. Cover them if necessary to keep them clean.

Tampons or sanitary pads are unlikely to be easily available except in big towns and menstruation can become irregular at altitude. For particularly heavy periods iron tablets might be advisable. Some doctors advise against the use of oral contraceptives at high altitudes because of increased risk of thrombosis. Pregnant women should obviously consult their doctor before going trekking.

The First Aid Kit
Given the above it is easy to set off carrying sufficient supplies for a small hospital, but a basic medical kit would include the following:

- Personal prescription medicines
- Plasters of various sizes, dressing tape
- Moleskin or other blister treatment
- 2 inch crepe bandage, elasticated bandage for sprains
- Codeine, paracetamol or Nurofen for pain relief and inflammation
- Antiseptic cream and high factor sunscreen and lip salve
- Lomotil or Immodium for diarrhoea and iodine for water purification
- Courses of 2 different broad spectrum antibiotics for dysentery and infection
- Tinidazole for Giardia, malaria suppressant and Diamox
- Scissors, needles, safety pins and tweezers

Other items you should consider are:
- Insect repellent and antihistamine cream, flea powder and thermometer
- Iron pills (for women)
- Nasal decongestants for colds
- Oil of cloves for toothache and antibiotic eye drops
- Rehydration sachets and anti-inflammatory cream
- Throat lozenges and cough drops
- AIDS kit. Many travellers today prefer to carry an AIDS pack

If you are travelling with several friends take a combined medical kit.

MEDICAL FACILITIES AND RESCUE

If you do have an emergency you will probably have to trek out to the nearest road. Unlike other Himalayan areas, in the Uttarakhand it is rare for you to be too far from a road, and since there is no formal rescue service you will need to look after yourself.

A casualty who is unable to walk will need to be carried out. If you have staff with you they should take the situation in hand, otherwise you should look to the local villagers for help. It is possible for porters to carry a casualty on their backs in relay, or using a basket cut into the shape of a seat. Mules are obviously the best choice. It is not possible to list all the medical facilities available here, but you will find hospitals in towns.

Only in the most extreme case should you consider a helicopter rescue. In many cases medical help will be reached more quickly by evacuation to the nearest road anyway. You should remember that rescues involve pilots in some risk. Only if you have an immovable casualty and there is absolutely no other alternative should you resort to asking for helicopter rescue and be prepared for delays.

You will need to send a message to the Indian Mountaineering Foundation, Benito Juarez Road, New Delhi through the nearest police or military post or the District Magistrate. You will be required to pay for the helicopter service. You must be sure your staff can deliver the message clearly, so write it out giving necessary details and accepting payment of the rescue expenses.

While the message is on its way the casualty should be moved to a suitable landing site, which should be marked so that the pilot can locate you. The international signals for help are to stand with your arms raised, a red flare or fire, or a square of red cloth. However, the use of any bright materials, mirrors and torches, or laying out sleeping bags and mats in a cross, are just as good. Your travel insurance policy should cover helicopter rescue costs, which are variable depending on flying time. Policies should also cover the costs of medical treatment and repatriation.

Helping The Local People

It is a common occurrence to be asked for medicine, and natural to want to help, but is not always a good idea. If you can help in a simple way, for example by giving codeine to a porter with a headache, then do so, but it is not advisable to go much beyond that unless you are a doctor and know what you are doing.

MAPS (Key to Maps p13)
There are very few maps of the Uttarakhand available, and none that is both detailed and accurate. The three Indian-produced trekking maps are of limited use, and any others are restricted from open sale within India for security reasons. If you are passing through Dehra Dun it is worth buying a copy of the available trekking maps from the office of the Survey of India, Maps Sale section, Hathibarkala.

The only maps of practical use for trekking in the Uttarakhand are two 1:200,000 sheets from the Indian Himalaya Map series, published by Leomann Maps under the editorship of Louis C. Baume. Sheet 7 is entitled Garhwal (Gangotri, Har-ki-Dun and Mussoorie), while sheet 8 is called Kumaon and Garhwal (Pindari Glacier, Badrinath and Nandadevi). Both have brief trek descriptions on the back, plus general information, relief maps and sketch maps of the main towns.

They are of a manageable size and clearly drawn, showing paths, rivers, ridges, peaks and glaciers. There are occasional errors, but these are relatively few and with all the trekking routes marked the maps are ideal. They cannot be relied on entirely but are recommended for use with this book. Different sources often give different heights for peaks or passes in the Garhwal, and places may have several names also. You can obtain both the Leomann and Huber maps from specialist map houses abroad.

THE TREKKER'S CODE
The following advice will ensure you do not cause offence, and enable you to mix easily with, and better understand, the people and pilgrims in Uttarakhand:

- Don't impose your values and standards on others. You are the visitor, you should adjust.
- Smile and spend time with the people you meet. If you have come only for the scenery you are missing out.
- Treat porters and others fairly. Do not lose your temper.

- Be responsible for your staff and equip them properly for the conditions.
- Don't rush around, carry too much, or go without a guide where one is recommended. Relax and enjoy.
- Make sure you are well equipped and insured.
- Look after your valuables and equipment.
- Bargain and try to pay a fair local rate for goods and services.
- Don't flash large sums of money around or give gifts too freely. Do so out of friendship or when deserved.
- Don't give drugs and medicines to the local people unless you are certain that it will not have any harmful effects.

The Adventure Tour Operator's Association have laid down the following guidelines to help preserve the environment and ancient culture of the Himalaya:

- Campsite: Remember that another party will be using the same campsite after you have vacated it. Therefore, leave the campsite cleaner than you found it.
- Limit deforestation: Make no open fires and discourage others from doing so on your behalf. Where water is heated by scarce firewood, use as little as possible. When possible choose accommodation that uses kerosine or fuel-efficient firewood stoves. You will help things greatly by taking with you some saplings and planting these on your trail.
- Burn dry paper and packets in a safe place. Bury other waste paper and biodegradable material including food. Carry back all non-biodegradable litter. If you come across other people's rubbish, remove their rubbish as well.
- Keep local water clean and avoid using pollutants such as detergents in streams or springs. If no toilet facilities are available, make sure you are at least 30m away from water sources and bury or cover waste.
- Plants should be left to flourish in their natural environment: taking cuttings, seeds and roots is illegal in many parts of the Himalaya.
- Help your guide and porters to follow conservation measures: Do not allow the cooks or porters to throw garbage in the nearby

stream or river.

The Himalaya may change you - please do not change them:

- Respect local traditions, protect local cultures, maintain local pride.
- When taking photographs, respect privacy: Ask permission and use restraint.
- Respect Holy places: Preserve what you have come to see, never touch or remove religious objects, remove shoes when visiting temples.
- Refrain from giving money to children or beggars since it will encourage begging: A donation to a project, health centre or a school is a better way to help.
- Respect local etiquette: Loose, lightweight clothes are preferable to revealing shorts, skimpy tops and tight fitting action wear. Hand holding or kissing in public are disapproved of by local people.

CHOOSING YOUR TREK

Some routes are more demanding than others. The transportation, distances, altitudes gained and what sort of demand a tour is likely to make on your capability are the considerations when choosing a trek. To help you further, I have graded the tours listed here. Remember that even if the walks are easy but duration of a trek is around two weeks, I would grade it 'B' or 'C' because its very length would put it into a more strenuous category.

Grade A: Pretty straightforward, food and accommodation readily available. Route obvious. Below 3000m elevation.

Grade B: Moderate, food and accommodation generally available. No guide required. Below 4000m.

Grade C: Bit strenuous or with snow on a few stretches. Food and accommodation available only on part of the route. Carrying tent essential. Guide optional except where recommended up to 4500m.

Grade D: Hard. Self-sufficiency and guide recommended. Above 4500m.

DISTANCES AND ALTITUDE

Measured distances are not a very important factor while describing a trekking route. On account of the nature of the terrain, and ascents and descents involved, it is more practical to describe a route in terms of time taken, including the time for reasonable rest. Here again the speed of a trekker will vary from person to person. I have occasionally given distances, in kilometres, but have mostly given the time taken based on average speed. It should be noted that overnight stopping places have been determined by availability of accommodation/campsite with water and views etc. Should the user want to divide the trek up differently the allocated times will give them enough information to do so. Altitudes have been given in metres where possible.

RESTRICTED AREAS

There are some parts of Garhwal and Kumaon Himalaya bordering Tibet and others, such as Nandadevi Sanctuary and Chakrata, which are restricted and no one is allowed to enter those areas without special permission from the Ministry of Home Affairs, New Delhi.

Principal treks are listed (see page 122). These include adjoining variations. Many treks link into others and the potential for combining them into extended routes is considerable. Some short treks have been included for the benefit of those who may be restricted by time or resources.

PINDARI GLACIER. GRADE B/C. 5 DAYS

Situated picturesquely along the south-eastern rim of Nandadevi Sanctuary. The Pinder river originates from this glacier. From the left bank of the lateral moraine grand views of Mt. Nandakhat (6611m), Nandakot (6860m), Pawali Dwar (6663m), Baljuari (5922m) and Changuch (6322m) are available. This is a very popular trek in Kumaon. Maximum height attained for viewing is 3820m. One can, however, go much higher.

Best Season: May-June and mid September to mid November.

Approach Route: The railhead is Kathgodam connected by North Eastern Railway with Delhi and Lucknow. Approach route from Dehra Dun is via Gwaldom and Bageshwar, almost the same distance as from Kathgodam. Regular public bus services are available. Private buses and taxis can also be chartered. Direct buses also operate between Delhi (starting from the Inter State Bus Terminus - ISBT) to Almora, Haldwani, Gwaldom and Nainital. Usually one service operates at night and one during the day from and to Delhi. Best advice is to check the latest times at the enquiry desk of U.P. Roadways, Delhi, by telephone. From Kathgodam you can reach Bageshwar, 182km, via Khairna in one day by public bus or taxi. It is advisable to spend the night here at the tourist bungalow. Bageshwar is a fast growing town on the confluence of the Gomti and Saryu rivers. If you decide to visit Nainital first, which is only 35km from Kathgodam, you can drive to Bageshwar, 138km, or to Song, 176km, the next day.

Day 2: In the morning drive to Song roadhead, 38km, and organise mules or porters if you need them, then trek 3km to Loharkhet. The 6km road to Loharkhet is due to be operational soon. Two-room tourist bungalows run by KMVN are available en route to Pindari glacier. You have to sleep on the floor if there are many visitors. Meals are also available in these bungalows. It is best to carry your

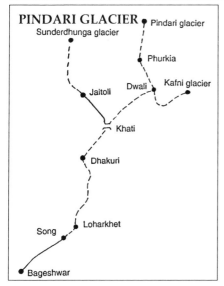

PINDARI GLACIER

It takes about 5 hours to get to this ridge. A further 20 minutes downhill is Dhakauri (2680m) with a tourist bungalow. Most travellers prefer to trek another 8km to Khati (2210m). This is the last village on this route. The well-made path from Dhakuri is gradual and downhill through forest. The trekking route to Sunderdhunga glacier forks a few kilometres, below Dhakuri, to the Umla-Jaitoli villages.

own tents. Loharkhet is a small village with a rest house and a private guest house.

Day 3: The trek on this day is steep and winding, rising over 1000m in 9km to Dhakuri pass (2900m) through oak and rhododendron forests. Remember to carry drinking water for the climb. The ridge provides a welcome excuse to stop for a while to admire the Nandakot range to the east and Maiktoli to the west.

Day 4: The route passes through dense forest including bamboo along the Pinder. You will notice some spectacular waterfalls across the rivers. Birdwatchers are likely to come across Hawk Cuckoo, Whistling Thrush, redstarts, wagtails, jays, Lammergier and Serpent Eagle. In about 5 hours you will reach Dwali (2575m). From here the route forks right to Kafni glacier along the Kafni river. Some prefer to spend a night here, others to continue a further 5km to Phurkia (3260m). The route from Dwali is rather steep and will take about 4 hours.

Day 5: Make an early start on a very gradual ascent through meadows. The treeline disappears a little away from Phurkia. As

123

you move on, lovely mountain views start appearing. In about 4 hours the zero point, the beginning of the glacier, at an altitude of 3820m, is reached. The rest of the day is yours to explore the glacier. It is 3km long and about 0.25km wide, formed by the vast quantities of snow off the lovely Baljuari, Nandakhat and Panwali range of peaks. You can also see Trails pass, named after a British officer who crossed it in 1930 trying to find a route into the Nandadevi Sanctuary. The view from the glacier of the high peaks is superb. Return journey to Phurkia takes about $2^{1/2}$ hours. From Phurkia you can either return to Khati conveniently in a day or make a side trip to Kafni glacier.

KAFNI GLACIER (3800m). GRADE C. 1/2 DAYS (see map p123) This beautiful glacier lies east of the Pinder valley under Mt. Nandakot. The route is well made and is worth a visit if you are equipped with tents. From Dwali turn east, following the Kafni river upwards through forest and meadows on a goat's trail. Byali, 10km, is a good campsite at 3570m and can be reached in 5 hours. From here the glacier and Nandikund are only 2km away, which you can explore the next day. Kafni provides grand views of Mt. Nandakot and Nandabhanar. With a bit of luck it should be possible to see Burrhel around Byali. If necessary a long day-return trip from Dwali to Kafni is possible.

SUNDERDHUNGA GLACIER (3860m). GRADE C. 3 DAYS (see map p123) It is possible to make yet another side trip to Sunderdhunga ('beautiful stones') glacier to the west of the Pinder valley. The route starts from Dhakuri or Khati villages. You need to have tents on this trek. Sunderdhunga is almost at the junction of the Sukhram and Maiktoli glaciers which take you right to the foot of Mt. Tharkot (6100m) and Maiktoli (6804m). Tharkot is a beautiful peak with a long ridge connecting it with Tent peak (looks like a tent), Nandakund, Bhanoti and Chakurijhaba. Other peaks in good view from the glacier would be Mrigthuni (6586m) and Panwali Dwar (6663m).
Day 1: Continue from Dhakuri or Khati (if you are returning from Pindari glacier) taking the route going down towards the

Sunderdhunga Gad river, through terraced fields and forests and across the river to reach Jaitoli, the last village en route (2400m), in about 6 hours. After crossing the river the uphill path passes through Wachham village. After Wachham there are a few short ascents and descents but mostly a level path to the village of Jaitoli, which will take $2^{1}/2$ hours. There are a few shops here and two simple guest houses providing meals where you may be able to replenish your stock of rice and flour. Seasonal vegetables and potatoes can be purchased in the village.

Day 2: On this day the route is through dense forest consisting of oak, bamboo and rhododendron. There is a campsite at Dhungyadong, 7km, which will take about 3 hours. The next campsite is Kathalia, 6km further, taking about 4 hours, but it is not advisable to push on straight to Kathalia (also called Sunderdhunga). The path immediately after Dhungyadong and about 3km further on is rather bad in two places, which consumes time and energy. It is therefore recommended to camp at Dhungyadong for the night.

Day 3: The route beyond Dhungyadong was badly damaged in a flood in 1995. A rope has to be fixed up at one point to cross a rocky face. It takes about 4 hours through forest to reach Sunderdhunga (Kathalia) (3500m), on the right side of the Sunderdhunga river. There is a tourist hut for shelter in bad weather. Across the river, above some shepherd huts, is the Maiktoli glacier (4200m). You can enjoy 2-3 days' exploration in this region by making Kathalia a base camp for day-return trips. If you have time shift your camp to the Sukram glacier by following the path above the tourist hut. After climbing about 600m, the path turns right towards the glacier. Close-up mountain views of Maiktoli, Tharkot and Mrigthuni peaks are available all the way. The entire area is very beautiful. It is also the route to Mt. Tharkot (6199m), the peak climbed in 1944 by C.W.F. Noice and Geoffrey Rawlinson. Nineteen years later the author led a team from Sherwood College, Nainital, to climb the peak.

PINDARI GLACIER, DEVAL EXTENSION. GRADE C. 6 DAYS
From Pindari glacier you can trek to either Bednibugyal meadows or Deval, roughly following the Pinder river. It is a strenuous but rewarding trek through villages, dense forests and meadows, with

Weaving

excellent mountain views. The trek starts from Khati. It is important to carry tents and engage a knowledgeable guide on this trek.

Day 1: Follow the path for about 1½ hours towards Dhakuri till you reach the tea house at Umla. Follow the path to your right through fields and forest to Gawali or Unyia school. It is a lovely walk on level path through the forest. The school at Unyia is reached in about 3 hours. Tents can be put up on the school ground with piped water and a grocery shop in the village. Another camping ground is available at Gwali, half an hour further on. Badyakot, a big prosperous village (2000m), is a further 4 hours. The school staff are very helpful and will let you put up tents in their grounds. There are a few shops to replenish provisions, and a few fresh vegetables may also be available. Much better would be to leave after lunch (you can buy a meal of rice and lentils in a tea house), and camp after about 1½ hours' uphill walk from the village in a nice meadow at 2600m with a spring for water, lovely views and fresh air in quiet surroundings. Remember that about half an hour after leaving the lower village, where the upper village commences there are two paths: one more conspicuous mule path up on your right, and a

126

goat's path up towards the left. I would recommend the left path with a guide as it is shorter to the next village and provides some adventure through dense forest.

Day 2: If you camped in the meadow on the previous day, the ridge will be reached in 15 minutes, followed by 2 hours' steep downhill through a dense forest to a stream at 1950m. The trail is visible but a bit slippery across rocks in one place. From the river it is uphill again through forest to the village of Bharakandi, taking a little over 2 hours. 25 minutes after crossing the river you come across some cultivated land and a shepherd hut. From here do not take the righthand uphill road; follow the lefthand path, which is a bit flat for a while, up to a stream and up again to the village. The primary school at Bharakanda (2330m) is at the upper end of the village. Head teacher Dayal Singh Danoo is very helpful and will be glad to offer you accommodation in the school. You can also pitch some tents in the grounds. There is plenty of running water and good views of the Som and Tatoni snow covered ranges.

Day 3: It is a short 4 hours uphill through forest to upper Mantoli Kharak at 3200m with a rewarding view of the Panchchuli range. An hour after leaving the village you will see a noticeboard in Hindi bearing the name of the roadbuilder. It provides great views of the Tharkot, Maiktoli and Mrigthuni ranges. There are a few shepherd huts about 10 minutes' walk beyond this beautiful spot. The upper meadow, called Mantoli Kharak, with just one hut close by and plenty of running water, is worth spending the whole day in. There is no suitable campsite with water for the next 4-5 hours.

Day 4: It is half an hour's steep uphill again up to the ridge. From the top the path is good and gradually downhill, except for 2-3 gentle climbs lasting not more than 10-15 minutes each. The views of the Panchchuli-Chiplakot range to the south-east and Mt. Trishul range in the north-west feast the eyes. Minchin, a shepherds' ground, is reached in about $2^{1}/_{2}$ hours. From here the good path on the right goes to Ghees village via Dalam Bodra, about 16km. The more adventurous path, however, is via Bagichi shepherd huts through dense forest. From Minchin take the downhill goat's track along the ridge leaving on your right the path for Dalam and Bodra. The trail is bit deceptive at several places, through dense forest, and takes about 6 hours from Minchin to Bagechi shepherd huts. The campsite far below the huts near the water point in the forest is recommended. Bagichi is one of the prettiest meadows in Uttarakhand, surrounded by virgin forest and the snow covered mountain ranges of Trishul and Nandaghunti.

Day 5: From Bagichi you could reach the roadhead at Deval in 3 days following the forest ridges via Nawali bugyal and Sawar village, linked to Deval by a jeepable road. However there will be very few locals who know this route, so it is recommended to walk down for about 3 hours to Ghees village via Dayalkhet shepherd huts and Sarmata village. The trail is well made. Do not plan to spend the night at Dayalkhet shepherd huts as the water point there disappeared in a huge landslide in 1994. Ghees at 1900m is a big prosperous village 200m above the Kail Ganga river with a few shops to replenish provisions. There is a good campsite at the old forest bungalow 2km from the village. From Ghees you can reach Bednibugyal meadow at 3354m in two stages via Balan village on the left bank of the Kailganga. Balan to Alibugyal is about a 1000m zigzag climb. If you wish to head for Deval, the 6ft wide well-made mule track is through pine forest. A few villages and tea houses are passed on the way. Most of the route is gradual downhill with the Kailganga flowing below. There is a tea house at Gurmtoli and some space to put up 2-3 tents with plenty of running water.

Day 6: Continue on the well-made path, along the Kailganga, reaching Suya and Agar village on the right bank of the river in about 2 hours, with a beautiful campsite by the river. Lasri village is reached in another 2 hours. It is situated by a bridge on the Kailganga and is midway to Swar and Deval, 7km each way by a jeep road, taking a little over 2 hours on foot across the Pinder river. There is a market, some simple eating places and a tourist bungalow at Deval.

MILAM & RALAM GLACIER TREK. GRADE B/C. 5 DAYS

Milam glacier, origin of the Goriganga river, is on the eastern approach to the Nandadevi Sanctuary and was open to foreigners only about 3 years ago. The trail passes through some of the gorgeous mountain scenery of Kumaon, partly through thick dark forests teeming with wildlife, with close-up views of not only the twin peaks of Mt. Nandadevi (7916m) but also many others such as

Nanda Kot (Photo: Author)
Trishul range from Mantoli Kharak (Photo: Author)

Mt Kalanog from Harkidoon trek (Photo: Author)
The Bhartokunta range (Photo: Author)

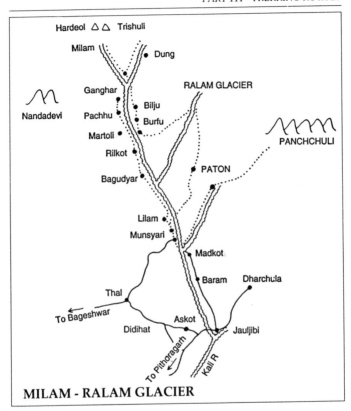

Hardeol △ △ Trishuli
Milam
Dung
Ganghar
Bilju
Nandadevi
Pachhu
Burfu
Martoli
Rilkot
Bagudyar
PATON
Lilam
Munsyari
Madkot
Baram
Dharchula
Thal
To Bageshwar
Askot
Didihat
Jauljibi
To Pithoragarh
Kali R
RALAM GLACIER
PANCHCHULI

MILAM - RALAM GLACIER

Hardeol and Trishuli.

For those who would like to do this trek without engaging a tour operator or porters, there are simple lodging places and basic cooked food available on the main route up to Milam village. This trek is on the Old Tibet route via Untadhura, Kingribingri pass (5564m). The Tibetan border is only about 25km from Milam village. No one, however, is allowed to go beyond Milam towards Tibet. The area between Munsyari, the starting point of the trek, and Milam on both sides of the Gori Ganga is called Johar valley. Once people from this valley did thriving trade with Tibet until 1959 when the trade route was closed for political reasons. Now most of the villages beyond Bogdyar are virtually deserted with only a few hardy inhabitants who move down to warmer places during winter. An effort is being made by the government to encourage the villagers to grow medicinal herbs, black cumin and a spice called Zimboo in the village above 2000m altitude. People from Johar are expert woollen carpet weavers.

The easiest approach to Milam glacier is from the present roadhead at Munsyari, a delightful little town providing a lovely close-up view of the five peaks of the Panchchuli, Rajrambha and Chiplakot ranges. The approach route to Munsyari is described elsewhere. A tourist bungalow under construction should now be ready and there are a few simple private guest houses. One such guest house with toilet and kitchen facilities belongs to Surendra Singh Pangtey. A very helpful and knowledgeable man in Kumaon Himalaya is Dr. Sher Singh Pangtey, a retired lecturer. Your mule and porter requirements should be arranged as far as possible in advance.

Munsyari

Foreigners are currently required to have passports checked at the office of the Sub Divisional Magistrate, Munsyari. There is a market to buy provisions and vegetables for the trip. Porters in this region are highly unreliable and their terms of service must be carefully negotiated. It is strongly recommended, if you have the time, to spend a day or two at Nainital in a comfortable hotel. The following stages are recommended assuming the availability of some accommodation/campsite and other facilities like water and eating places.

Day 1: It is a short 4 hours' easy trek, about 6km downhill via Darkot village to Suring Gaad, a hydroelectric station, on the banks of the Gori Ganga. Follow the river upwards on a very well maintained mule track to Jimi Ghat, 3km, with a school, a few shops and a police checkpost. Lilam (1900m) is 3km further. There is a small camping place and a few tin huts with piped water. This place used to be a camp for paramilitary forces but was severely damaged by a huge landslide a couple of years ago. What is left of the camp now is quite safe. Paton village is across the river - you pass through Paton on the way back from Ralam glacier.

Day 2: There used to be a lovely path along the bank of the Gori Ganga to Bogdyar, 12km, but it was washed away in several places, leaving sheer rocks, in the unprecedented floods of 1995. A new path was under construction and should now be functional. If not, a temporary road has been built through Lilam village which entails over 3 hours' steep uphill to an altitude of 3200m and then about 1000m downhill to join the old path to Bogdyar (2400m). In all this takes 9 hours including time for a hot meal on the way. Bogdyar is a small place with a police checkpost, a few shops and a three-room Public Works Department rest house which is always in great demand. A few tents can be put up alongside the rest house.

Day 3: Follow the obvious mule path along the Gori Ganga. A few minutes after leaving the camp it zigzags up for about 45 minutes when it virtually touches the river by the side of a temple below a steep rock face. In May there will be accumulated avalanched snow in a couple of places through which a path should have been carved out by the Public Roadbuilders. The tea house at Mapang is reached in about 4 hours. You can either buy a meal of rice and lentils at the tea house or do your own cooking. It is a lovely place for a rest. There is an old path about half a kilometre before reaching Mapang, carved out across a hard rockface just above the river with holes made on the rock to hold logs. Planks are put over the logs like a hanging bridge for the path. This dangerous path is used only by locals now, as a safer route going a bit higher, down to Mapang, has been made over the rockface. About 2km further after crossing the Lapa stream you leave the path on the left which goes to Laspa village, 2km uphill towards the Shalang glacier originating from Nandakot, and continue following the Gori Ganga about 3km further to the village of Rilkot. Most of the houses at Rilkot are deserted but there is a tea house and a Border Police Post. It is a very windy place. You are advised to camp about 15 minutes' walk further on in a meadow below a rockface with small caves, before starting the ascent. It is a bit sheltered from the winds, which die down around 6pm. Make sure to carry kerosine oil on this route as firewood is not available at several places.

Day 4: After the first ascent of about 45 minutes, the old ruined village of Rilkot is passed. About half an hour further, the lefthand path goes to the interesting village of Martoli, about 2km (3385m). The lower path goes to Burfu and Milam. Across the river you can see the villages of Tola and Samdu connected by a shaky log bridge over the Gori Ganga. It is recommended to take the Martoli route through lovely flower studded slopes for the view of Mt. Nandakot. This is also the approach route to the Lawan glacier and the base camps for Mt. Nandakot and Nandadevi East. Martoli is a very windy village, the winds howling from about 8am to 6pm. In fact the entire Goriganga valley and villages both sides of the river are windy. There is a very well preserved birch forest above Martoli village with the temple of Nanda Devi just below the forest. You can very usefully spend a day or two here exploring the meadows to the east of the forest for splendid mountain views. The mostly deserted village is spread out all along the ridge. There is a shop to cater for basic needs during the season. A fair is held here during the first half of September at the Nandadevi temple. The valley is famous for growing good quality potatoes. For the more adventurous a route via Trails pass (6000m) through dangerous icefalls leads to the Pindari glacier. From Martoli join the main path to Milam, walk past the village down the ridge to the log bridge over the Lwa river, 10 minutes downhill. From here Burfu is only about an hour across the Goriganga. The big village of Burfu (3370m) on the left bank of the river is about 10 minutes' walk uphill from the main path and the bridge. There are 2-3 shops here. Through wind and dust you continue to Bilju village, 3km, and to Milam (3650m), a further 3km. As you cross Bilju a lovely view of the northern face of Nandadevi appears. The villages over on the right side of the river are Pachhu to the right with Ganghar on its left. Just before reaching Milam you cross a bridge over the Gunkha river, which originates from the watershed of Tibet. Milam is the village of Pandit Nain Singh Rawat, who in the 19th century surveyed Tibet disguised as a Lama. His grandson H.C.S. Rawat climbed Mt. Everest in 1965. Other important personalities from this village are S.S. Pangtey, a senior bureaucrat of the Indian Administrative Service, and the late Hukum Singh, a celebrity mountaineer and retired Deputy Director General of the Indo-Tibetan Border Police. There is a Border Police Check (foreigners required to show passports), a P.W.D. Inspection bungalow, which can be used by tourists, a post office, 2-3 shops and a small guest house. It is a very interesting village.

Day 5: You can make a return trip to Milam glacier (3700m), source of the Gori Ganga, which takes about 4 hours, to view Hardeol (7151m) and Trisuli (7440m). There used to be a lovely route through the left lateral moraine of the Milam glacier to Sandalya Kund (4200m), virtually touching the glacier forming out of the Hardeol and Tirsuli icefalls, giving a thrilling experience. Unfortunately a huge landslide has made this approach inaccessible. Nevertheless it is still worthwhile to go with a packed lunch and a guide to the farthest point possible and enjoy the glory of nature. The day trip can conveniently be made in 7 hours.

EXTENSION TO PACHHU GLACIER. GRADE C. 8 HOURS

If you have time, you must not miss a trip to Pachhu glacier with a guide. It takes you right to the foot of the northern face of Nandadevi, with an unforgettable close-up view of the peaks. The approach route is from the bridge on the Gori Ganga at Burfu, keeping to the right bank of the river. From the bridge Ganghar village is about 2 hours' walk, on the right bank of Pachhu stream. You can either spend the night at Ganghar or continue for another 2½ to 3 hours, roughly along the right bank of the Pachhu on a goat's trail to Pachhu meadows (4100m), just where the birch forest ends by the side of a stream. Soon after leaving Ganghar, following the water pipeline upward, the Nandadevi range starts to reveal itself, feasting your eyes with the glorious view. At two places large landslides have to be crossed. They are not too dangerous but you need to be surefooted. The meadows, streams and the forest passed through are a great source of pleasure.

EXTENSION TO RALAM GLACIER. GRADE C/D. 4 DAYS

This extension has been included for more psychological than scenic satisfaction. It involves 4 hours' steep uphill climb followed by 4 hours' nasty downhill across the 4500m Bridge-Gang pass, which can be very tiring. You must be self-sufficient in all respects.

Day 1: Starting from Burfu, Tola village is 3km on the left bank of the Gori Ganga via a goat's path. From Tola go down to the Tola gad stream, taking about 20 minutes, cross the river over a log bridge and head north-west, keeping the stream to your left, passing through the remains of a shepherd hut, and start climbing up. In about 2¹/₂ hours a nice place for camping with plenty of deadwood and water is available. This place can also be reached in a day from Milam. The pass is another 2 hours from here with a campsite near a shepherd hut below the pass. Do not attempt to cross the pass after 5pm because there is no camping place with water down the other side of the pass for about 2¹/₂ hours.

Day 2: Set out early to cross the pass and enjoy the mountain views which extend from the Milam glacier region to Ralam glacier. The steep downhill trek to Ralam village takes about 4 hours. There is a small campsite about 15 minutes from the village en route to the glacier, which is only about 2 hours from the village. The villagers are very hospitable and will be glad to offer you room in their low roofed, smoky houses. They enjoy local brews. With a little persuasion they will entertain you with local songs and folk dances. If they entertain you, you should reciprocate by buying them a couple of bottles of the local brew.

Day 3: From Ralam the return journey is via Sapa Udyar (cave) and Paton village, joining the Milam glacier route at Lilam. The route is mostly downhill through meadows and partly dense forest. If you have porters, you may have to spend the night in Sapa Udyar, a protected shelter under a huge rock which has at least a metre deep of goat's droppings accumulated in the cave and is large enough to accommodate ten 2-man tents and over 100 goats!

Day 4: From Sapa Udyar the path follows a stream for a while though forest then climbs for about 2 hours, and another hour downhill, to the village of Paton where you can cook your lunch and see woollen carpets being made in the village. From here the bridge over the Goriganga is about half an hour downhill to Lilam. You can spend a night 3km further down at Jimighath, in the primary school or one of the tea houses, arriving at Munsyari the following day in time for lunch.

MILAM TO NITI VALLEY VIA UNTA DHURA PASS (5377m).
GRADE D. 7 DAYS

A most challenging and fascinating traverse from Milam to Malari (3021m) in the Niti valley of Garhwal is via the Unta Dhura and Sumna (4520m) passes. This route falls in the restricted area and permission has to be obtained from the Ministry of Home Affairs to do this trek. Also you need to go self-contained in all respects. The route is feasible only for a brief period from mid June to early October. With improved relations between India and China, it may be possible in a few years for the Indian government to remove the restriction and allow Indian and foreign parties to do this exciting trek. It will take 7 days from Milam to Malari via Dung, Topidhunga, Chhedang, Lapthal and Sumna.

KALI AND KUTI VALLEYS TO CHHOTA KAILASH (6191m). GRADE C/D.

This is another challenging trek in Kumaon, commencing at Tawaghat, the roadhead from Pithoragarh via Dharchula. There are, however, doubts as to whether or not the existing rules permit Indians and foreigners to do this trek without obtaining special permission. Anyone interested in doing the trek is advised to contact the District Magistrate, Pithoragarh, for guidance. The route takes you to the confluence of the Kali and Kuti rivers at Gunji and then to Jonlingkong, Parvati tal (lake) and chhota Kailash, with lovely close-up views of the glacier and mountain ranges of Api and Nampa. The engravings on the houses and temples in the Kuti valley are fascinating and the people very friendly. You will need to take tents and provisions on this trek.

MUNSYARI-KHALYA TOP TREK. GRADE B. 3 DAYS

You can enjoy three days of easy trekking to Khalya top (3650m), a beautiful meadow providing grand views of the Kalabaland, Hansling, Panchchuli and Chiplakot ranges. Porters can be hired at Munsyari. It can be undertaken between March and November, and tents and provisions will have to be taken.

Day 1: The porters will help you find the shortest route leaving the motorway from Munsyari to Banati farm, which takes about 3 hours and is a lovely spot to enjoy your picnic lunch. It is uphill all the way, partly through forest. From Banati farm continue through the forest to Bhujeni, a shepherd camp 2 hours uphill and a good spot for camping at about 3000m.

Day 2: After an hour's climb, there is a lovely walk along the ridge for a short while and then half an hour's fairly level path to the

Khalya shepherd huts at 3350m. You can continue climbing up the ridge to the highest point, called Khalya top. It is a lovely walk through meadow with great views. Come down to the Khalya shepherd huts for the night.

Day 3: The return to Munsyari will take at most four hours, downhill all the way, leaving you enough time to organise your transport for the onward journey.

THE TREK TO RUPKUND (THE MYSTERY LAKE). GRADE C. 5 DAYS

Season: May to November. Snow above 3350m in May, early snow in November. Snow around Rupkund throughout the year. July/ August wet but best for flowers.

The Mystery Lake: Rupkund (meaning lake of images) is an oval-shaped glacial lake set in a deep hollow below the ridge of Mt. Chandnikot into the south-west of Mt. Trishul at 5029m. Due to its height and sheltered position the lake is frozen over for most of the year and thaws out for a few weeks in July-August. It is only about 200m in circumference (though some describe it as larger), and is no deeper than about 5m. It is not the natural beauty of the lake which draws trekkers (there are many more attractive lakes in Uttarakhand) but the stories surrounding its 'mystery'. These concern some skeleton remains found by a local forester when visiting the lake in 1942. From the remains it is estimated that over 300 people died from exposure in this remote spot 400-500 years ago, and although it is assumed they died when trapped in bad weather, there are several explanations for the mystery of why they were there in the first place. There is little credibility in stories of traders as the trail leads nowhere. One popular myth goes that they were soldiers returning from a mission in Tibet, and that there are still trails of skeletons, still in armour, entombed in the ice, with weapons strewn about. However the myth has no basis in fact and the route is nowhere connected with the approach to Tibet. The truth is probably that they were a party of pilgrims undertaking the Nandajat yatra to Homkund, another lake beyond Rupkund. The pilgrimage still takes place today (see later), and local villagers preserved this tale in a song which was forgotten until the rediscovery of the remains caused it to be revived.

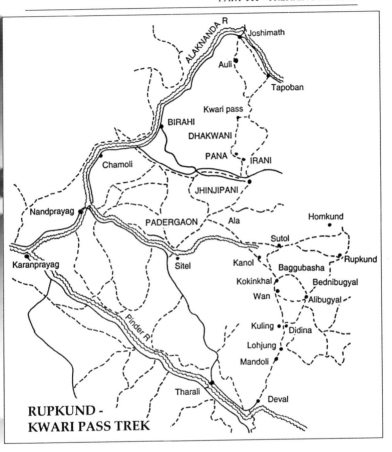

RUPKUND -
KWARI PASS TREK

According to the local folk songs, Raja Jasdev of Kanauj undertook
a Nanda Jat, together with Rani Balwa. Rani, being a princess from
Garhwal, was revered as a sister of the goddess Nandadevi. Near
Rupkund she gave birth to a baby. Nandadevi considered it a
sacrilege in her domain and sent down a snow storm. Raja's people
were caught in it and perished. Since no one will ever be sure what
happened, Rupkund will remain 'The Mystery Lake', but trekkers

should not go with a view to finding the grim remains which sparked off the mystery! The few scattered bones that are there are no attraction, and they are only exposed for a few short weeks during the thaw.

Although Rupkund makes an interesting destination the real attraction is the magnificent scenery you trek through to reach it. This area between the Pinder river and the Nandakini (which has Homkund as its source) has interesting villages and pine forests but it is particularly renowned for its Bugyals (meadows), the mountain panoramas which are spectacular even by the standards of Garhwal. The area is also especially rich in mountain flora. There are shelters available all along the route, but they can be primitive and sometimes used by animals. It is best to take a tent. A guide is particularly recommended in May when the path will be hidden beneath snow from Bednibugyal on.

Access: The trek begins in the Pinder valley, with access via Gwaldom or Tharali. Buses leave the Kumaon hill station Almora in the morning for Gwaldom via Bageshwar. For those coming from Garhwal, a better approach route, you take the road to Tharali via Karanprayag. Buses leave Dehra Dun and Rishikesh early in the morning and arrive at Tharali around 4pm.

Day 1: Gwaldom (1830m) or Tharali (1300m) are the recommended starting points. There is a thriving bazar for last-minute supplies and simple accommodation at either a private guest house or the tourist bungalow at Gwaldom. The views across the Pinder valley to Trishul at the start of your trek are spectacular and inspiring. The walk down through fragrant Chir pines to the bridge at Nandakesri across the Pinder, and then on to the village of Debal, is very worthwhile. It is an easy 7km walk down to the river, passing two villages on the way, and a further 2km along the valley to Debal (4 hours total). You could use local transport on the new road which now links Gwaldon and Debal, but it is better to walk. From Tharali public buses or jeep taxis are available to Deval, 13km, and further to Lohjung, 18km. I would not recommend a walk from Tharali to Deval on the metalled road. Since Tharali has neither basic accommodation for tourists nor any suitable campsite, it is advisable to hire a jeep taxi to Deval, where simple accommodation in the marketplace and a tourist bungalow 2km before the village are available, or to Lohjung. The drive is through an attractive valley along the Pinder. The river is famous for trout fishing. As you approach Deval, Nandaghunti and Trishul can be seen higher up. Historically, Gwaldom was a major stopping point for the explorers and mountaineers heading towards Nandadevi in the early part of the century. Most of their accounts mention the hard climb up to what was then the only Dak Bungalow on the route, and praise the view. The main route from Gwaldom across the Kuari pass to Joshimath is also known as the Curzon Trail, after Lord Curzon who trekked the route when he was a viceroy. The trek to Rupkund is really a deviation off this route.

Day 2: Deval to Lohjung or Mundoli is 14km on foot and takes about 6 hours. You walk on a dusty road through several villages. It is gently uphill all the way except for the last $1^1/_2$km from Bagrigad through Mundoli village, which is rather steep. There are tea houses at several places where a meal of rice and lentils can be purchased. Mundoli is a big village with a post office and a dispensary, but it cannot be relied on for essential supplies. Lohjung is a pass of 2250m where a few shops, two simple guest houses and a tourist bungalow have sprung up. Khadak Singh, owner of one of the guest houses, is a helpful man. You get an excellent view of Mt. Nandaghunti (6309m) to the north-east. There are two small temples and two big bells hanging from a tree on the col. If you have time it is well worth climbing to the top of the eastern ridge called Archan Dhar. It takes 45 minutes to this lovely place, through silver oak and rhododendron forest with a panoramic view of distant mountain ranges and of the valley below up to Gwaldom.

Those short of time can use transport from Gwaldom, Tharali or Deval to reach Lohjung. However, during the monsoon this road is mostly closed to traffic due to landslides. From Deval you can also follow the left bank of the Pinder to reach Alibugyal and Bednibugyal meadows in 3 days via the villages of Ghees and Balan. This route is described elsewhere.

Day 3: Again there is a choice of routes but the easiest and most frequented is through the large village of Wan (2439m). The alternative is via Didina (2560m). You can see both villages in the valley from Lohajung, Didina being across the Raunagad river to the north-east (right).

It is an easy walk to Wan as you take the obvious trail along the Raunagad river (also called the Bedni Ganga) following the broad mule track along the valley, crossing two streams en route. You start off with about 2 hours' gradual descent to the shepherd huts and a watermill. From the watermill a path going up to your left leads to the village of Kuling, taking about 45 minutes. For Wan continue on the trail across the stream for about 1km further. The main route goes up to the left, along the west bank of the river, to Wan, 5km. The righthand trail goes downwards to Didina across the Raunagad river.

The path is pleasantly shaded by mixed forest including gnarled Himalayan oak, pine and rhododendron but it leaves the river shortly before Wan. The village is well spread out and its houses fill the valley floor. Villagers here still wear a thick homespun blanket folded around them as a versatile cloak. There is a tourist bungalow here, and also a forest rest house which is set in a clearing above the village to the east ridge and is hidden from sight. Beside it is the temple, dedicated to local deity Latoo, set beneath a huge deodar pine. An annual festival is held in the temple in June/July. You may find a few supplies here - this is the last chance to do so - or a local to guide you up to Rupkund. It will not be possible to buy cooked meals from now on.

The alternative and more scenic route is to take the right fork 1km beyond the watermill and cross the Raunagad river by a bridge before climbing a well-made zigzag path up to Didina village, where you can stay in the school. If you are camping it is best to take the path beside the village and climb up to Tolpani (2 hours), which is a clearing in the forest with some shepherd huts. Near the village the trail is not very clear so it is best to ask the way. There is a stream nearby at Tolpani, and wild strawberries are in abundance on this route during June-July.

Day 4: This is 6km of steep ascent from Bednibugyal (3354m). It takes $4^1/_2$ hours with plenty of time for exploration on arrival. From the tourist bungalow cross the stream and climb the east (right) side of the valley up the ridge which now separates you from the Raunagad river. Follow the track back down to the river and from the bridge take the well-made mule track which climbs up through dense forest to Bednibugyal. There are many animal tracks in the forest, but the main path is very clear. After a long climb you emerge from the forest onto the lower slopes of Bednibugyal and traverse the hillside towards two forestry huts with pointed roofs. (The locals have also built two tourist shelters which accommodate about 20.) As you do so the full extent of the meadows and the panoramic view open up to you. The huts are well built but may be soiled by animals or already occupied by local shepherds. Nearby you will find a small manmade lake called Bedni Kund, and two small temples with bells and a carved stone statue inside. The villagers from Wan hold a festival here at Bedni Kund every July/ August to thank the goddess of the meadows for protecting their livestock. An annual cultural festival is held here in early September attended by over 1500 people from villages as far as 15km away.

It is certainly best to camp in the huge area of flower-studded meadow around you. The treeline is 175m below and the whole horizon ahead is filled with the mountains of Eastern Garhwal. Very close on the right are Trishul and Nandaghunti and then comes the conical looking Neelkanth, the great walls of Chaukhamba and beyond that Kedarnath peak. If you have plenty of time it is the perfect place to spend a couple of days exploring the surrounding area and enjoying the magnificent views from several viewpoints. At any rate, as it is a long hard ascent from here to Rupkund, it is a good idea to spend at least one day here to acclimatise.

From Tolpani take the trek just above the huts and climb for an hour through bamboo and rhododendron forest to a col on the ridge, where you will get a first view of the Badrinath peaks. Follow the ridge up to your left and as you gradually climb the views become more and more extensive, revealing the peaks of the Mt. Nandakot range on the east, and you enter open meadow. In summer hundreds of sheep, goats and horses will be grazing here. In a further 2 hours you arrive at Ali Bugyal and join the route from Ghees and Balan. The last British Deputy Commissioner of Garhwal, Verneed, was so fond of this area that he built a hut here and, although it is now ruined, old shepherds still call it Verneed's hut. From here the well-made path gradually zigzags uphill to the top of Bednibugyal. It takes $1^{1}/_{2}$ hours from Alibugyal. On reaching the saddle on the ridge descend to your left towards the two forestry huts, leaving the main path, which continues on to Rupkund.

141

Day 5: You can make the 12km return trip to Rupkund (5029m) in 10 hours. It is a very hard but very rewarding day. If you are finding the going tough, or are not acclimatising well to the altitude, you should not attempt the return trip. The alternatives are either to go to Bagubasha on the first day, then trek to Rupkund and return to Bednibugyal, or to visit Rupkund and return to Bagubasha for the night. You may see Monal, snow partridges, or the rare blue mountain sheep in this area. The path is very clear up to Bagubasha and after that reasonably clear.

From the Bednibugyal lake climb for about 25 minutes to join the path from Ali Bugyal. Follow this for an hour across the ridge to a small col. You can go to Wan or the village of Kanol via the left path, which is rather long but has excellent views. The path to the right traverses the slope towards Rupkund.

The path now contours the slope, then climbs steeply up through the meadows of Patar Nachanni (3658m). The name means 'place of the dancing girls' and refers to a legend that the Raja of Kanauj camped here while on pilgrimage. In his entourage he had three dancing girls. When they performed three holes opened up in the ground and swallowed them, and they were never seen again. You will pass the three holes referred to in the legend, each about $5^{1/2}$ft deep.

At the top of the climb is Kalwavinayak, where there is a stone statue of the elephant god Ganesh (4 hours from Bednibugyal). There is a superb view of Mt. Nanda Ghunti and Rupkund from here, with Mt. Trishul rising dramatically above them. In 1907 Trishul became the highest peak in the world to have been climbed when Dr T.G. Longstaff made his remarkable ascent, going from 5334m to the summit in one day. It wasn't until 1930 that a higher summit was reached.

After another 15 minutes' level going you reach Bagubasha (cave of the tiger) where you can shelter in the rough cave. There are also four or five low huts. From here it is a steep and sometimes difficult ascent to Rupkund, which is at the head of the valley. The trail can be indistinct or snow covered, but the location of the lake between the steep ridges that form the valley, is obvious enough. Depending on acclimatisation the climb takes around $2^{1/2}$ hours.

Above the lake on the lefthand side of the ridge is Mt. Chandnikot

(5055m). A trail from the right side of the lake climbs straight up to the ridge of Jiunragali (5135m) in about 45 minutes. From here you get the best close-up view of Trishul's three summits across the Shilashaudra glacier. The climb is worthwhile for that reason alone.

The name Jiunragali, 'Col of destruction', is again associated with the ill-fated Raja of Kanuj as some of his party are said to have died here in a storm created by the vengeful goddess Nandadevi. The legend is probably connected with the mysterious bones lying below in the lake. The grim nature of the local legends in this area is not surprising as many pilgrims must have died of cold and exposure in this mountain terrain in years gone by. If nothing else they serve as a constant reminder to the trekker to take care.

Beyond the ridge you can continue about 1500m down to the snout of the glacier and on up to Homkund (4061m) but this is another difficult day's trek (13km). It is possible to descend down the Nandakini river from Homkund to the roadhead at Ghat (1331m) via the village of Sitel (4 days), but the trail is not marked and a guide from Wan or Kuling should be taken for this trek. The road from Ghat joins the Badrinath highway at Nandprayag.

Nandajat (Nanda Raj Jat)

Homkund is the destination of pilgrims to this area, who travel there to worship the goddess Nandadevi. Every twelve years the Nanda Raj Jat pilgrimage takes place, starting from the village of Nauti, 25km from Karanprayag. It is said that a four-horned ram is born to the village flock a year before the pilgrimage and this ram leads the way as the procession continues slowly through the hills, gathering more pilgrims, and with much blowing of horns and beating of drums. Offerings are placed in a pouch and fastened to the back of the ram. There are special ceremonies at the temples at Wan and Bednibugyal. The district administration helps in providing some tents, food and medical facilities to the pilgrims, where these are scarce. Otherwise the villages en route provide hospitality. According to the divine instruction of Nandadevi, there is a custom in Wan village of keeping everyone's house unlocked for use by the pilgrims on the day of their arrival. When the party finally reaches Homkund the ram is said to disappear with tears in its eyes, a sign that the goddess has accepted the offerings.

There are no historical records but it is gathered from local folklore and folksongs (Jagar) that in the 9th century the Raja Shalipal, who had his capital at Chandpurgarh, 'installed' the goddess Nandadevi (Raj Rajeshwari) at the village Nauti, and the royal priest or Nautiyal was made responsible by the people of Nauti village for regular worship of the goddess. The King also started the Nanda Raj Jat. Later, his younger brother Ajaipal Kunwar, settled at Kansuwa village nearby, was authorised to organise the pilgrimage on behalf of the King. Traditionally descendants of Kunwar come to Nauti to seek the blessing of Nandadevi to organise the pilgrimage. A timetable is organised by the priests so that the pilgrimage reaches Homkund on the Nandastmi (an auspicious day) in August/September and Kulsari on the preceding new moon for special worship.

The Goddess Nandadevi

According to the Puranas, Mahadev or Lord Shiva's marriage to Parvati, also known as Nandadevi, daughter of the Himalaya, was solemnised in the Garhwal Himalaya. They have always lived in the Himalaya, which is why many mountains and rivers are associated with the name Nanda, and there are many Nandadevi temples in Garhwal and Kumaon. It is believed the marriage took place at Homkund.

Like the Panwar dynasty of Garhwal, the Chand dynasty of Kumaon also worshipped Nandadevi as their family deity. In both regions, daughters, sisters and fathers' sisters are considered idols of the goddess Nandadevi and as such are called 'Dhyani'. The Nandajat pilgrimage is also connected with the village tradition in Uttarakhand whereby the married daughter is given a traditional send-off to her inlaws' place.

Raja Udyot Chand (1678-98) had a temple dedicated to Nandadevi built at Almora, which was removed during British rule by Trail, the then commissioner of Garhwal and Kumaon. It is said that after removing the temple Trail went on an expedition in the Nandadevi region, during which he became blind. The locals advised him to restore the Nandadevi temple at its original place. When it was done, his sight was restored. The goddess Nandadevi is also called 'Shakti' or power. The Puranas believe that the invincible power, or 'Mahashakti', is present in the Himalaya in the form of the goddess Nandadevi. In the old days there was a custom of suffixing the first name of a girl with 'Devi', eg. Kamladevi.

SIDE TRIP TO VIKALTAL LAKE AND BRAHMTAL RIDGE (3250m). GRADE B. 4 DAYS

If you go up to Rupkund from Lohjung via Didina, as recommended, the return to Lohjung should be made via the villages of Wan and Kuling from Bednibugyal. A fit person can do this in one day as most of the 18km route is downhill. Alternatively start late from Bednibugyal after enjoying the morning views and spend the night at Wan, $3^{1}/_{2}$ hours, or Kuling, $2^{1}/_{2}$ hours further. Kuling is an interesting village with a school for accommodation.

A Primary Health Centre is under construction here by a non-government social service organisation called CHETNA-GARA (General Awareness In Rural Areas), of which the author is a founder patron. The Centre will be run as a result of financial support from trekker friends from the UK and the CHETNA-GARA in Australia, under the leadership of Dr Sabina Obermeder. Efforts are being made to develop the Centre as a model village, and the doctor of the Centre or the village head will be glad to arrange your accommodation.

From Kuling to Lohjung takes $2^{1}/_{2}$ hours. From Lohjung you can make an interesting 4-day trek to Tharali via Vikaltal lake (2900m) and Brahmtal ridge, with lovely mountain views.

Day 1: Follow the ridge route from above the Nandadevi guest house, reaching the upper Mundoli village in about half an hour. From here the route turns left along the waterpipe line, gradually ascending by a narrow path. The trail is quite clear but a guide would be helpful to show you the water point, a suitable campsite and the route to Tharali. Most of the route is through bamboo, oak, deodar and rhododendron forest.

It is a pleasant walk. After crossing the third stream the last ascent of about half an hour ends at some shepherd huts perched on a ridge, with space for a few tents. Vikaltal lake (a dark-water lake with a religious story associated) is ten minutes further on. A lovely campsite can be found about an hour's walk uphill, in a meadow with clear views of Mt. Trishul and the Badrinath range of peaks.

There is a year-round water spring which fills a bucket in about 10 minutes during summer and is about 10 minutes' walk from the camp - an inconvenience more than compensated by the excellent views.

Day 2: You can spend the day enjoying the views on short walks or follow the path along the ridge towards Talanti (3340m), the highest point of the ridge, as far as you can. It is a delightful walk along the ridge with panoramic views. In March-April the rhododendrons are in bloom. This can be a very rewarding trek to those with only a few days at their disposal and can be done during March-April or November-December.

Day 3: Walk down to the shepherd huts you passed the previous day, with a muddy pond, and take the path above the pond down the left ridge through forest. It is mostly downhill and a very pleasant route. It takes about 7 hours to reach the upper village of Kurad, called Bajwar, which has a few shops and a lovely campsite with piped water. It is a remote area, so you may not see anyone else on the path.

Day 4: From Bajwar, walk down through the big, scattered village of Kurad to Tharali, 2 hours, and take transport back to Dehra Dun, arriving in about 8 hours.

KWARI PASS. GRADE C/D

Best time: May-June and mid September-October. The Nandadevi Sanctuary is set in a magnificent group of over 60 peaks around Mt. Nandadevi (7817m) including Chhangbhang (6866m), Trishul (7120m), Mrigthuni (6855m), and Nandakot (6863m). Parallel with the main range lies a massive mountain block extending from Dunagiri (7066m) in the north to Trishul in the south, and between these two lies a rough parallelogram about 10km long and 7km wide with a narrow and precipitous cliff through which the Rishi Ganga has carved its way. The approach to the back of these mountains, the Nandadevi Sanctuary, is very difficult.

W. Grahm, a Swiss guide, was the first European to explore this region in 1883, followed by Tom Longstaff in 1907. This region was popular for climbing before the second world war and was made famous by the explorations of Eric Shipton and Bill Tilman, culminating in the climbing of Mt. Nandadevi by Tilman and Odell

Shepherd at Bhunna

in 1936. For many years this remained the highest-climbed mountain in the world. The view from the Nandadevi Sanctuary is one of the best in the world. Unfortunately trekkers, climbers and locals alike are not permitted at present to enter the sanctuary, for environmental reasons. The inner sanctuary via the Rishi gorge is closed but the area to the west of the Nandadevi group is superb walking country. It affords magnificent views of the Nandadevi and Badrinath peaks, which between them include virtually all of Garhwal's highest peaks and is open for trekking without a special permit. The best way to enjoy this trek is to follow part of the approach route from Gwaldom to Kwari pass used by Shepton and Tilman for the ascent of Nandadevi, and used by Lord Curzon also. Details of Gwaldom/ Tharali and the route up to Wan are described elsewhere. Time permitting, if you are returning from Rupkund you can continue to Kwari pass (6265m) and Joshimath. Another shorter approach route to Kwari pass is to take a bus or taxi from Nandprayag to Ghat, 19km, and walk via Ramni village to Semkharak in one day. The route from Wan also joins here and is described below.

Day 1: Take the route above the forest rest house, keeping the Latoo temple on your right. The path is quite clear and goes to your left

147

above Wan village, via rhododendron, oak and chestnut forest, to the Kokinkhal pass (3121m) in about 2 hours. There is a fascinating route from Bednibugyal via Bhunna, about 18km, which also arrives here, but you would need a guide for it. It follows the ridge opposite Bednibugyal, with views of Trishul, Nandaghunti, and Bethartoli (6352m). The night stop after Bednibugyal will be the shepherd huts at Bhunna.

From Kokinkhal you climb a 600m ridge towards the west, with views of the central Himalayan peaks. You can reach Kanol for the night, which is only 1¹/₂ hours downhill. There is a good campsite and a forest rest house at Kanol (2150m). The main village is about 1¹/₂km down the road to Sitel. Basic provisions are generally available in the shop. You will do well to replenish your stocks either at Wan or Kanol. These two villages are also the major suppliers of trekking porters who can be relied on to know the path, although some of them, particularly from Kanol, can be difficult. From Kanol you can reach Ghat roadhead in two stages for transport to Rishikesh, etc.

Day 2: From Kanol the commonly used all weather route is via Sutol village, 8km, 2¹/₂ hours. The path is below the forest rest house to your right. After 200m the path forks: take the lower path. It goes through dense deodar and chestnut forest, and in one or two places is a bit confusing. About an hour after leaving Kanol, take the path to your right, which looks a bit more level, leaving the downhill path. It will take you to the bridge on the Nandakini river, which has watermills and a good place to camp. The interesting village of Sutol is across the river, with a primary school and two shops. (The shopkeepers are rarely in their shops during the day as the villagers do their shopping in the morning before going to work or in the late evening.) Trekkers returning from Homkund, described in the Rupkund trek, will join the road here and continue to the roadhead at Ghat, 16km, a downhill journey via Sitel. (Do not confuse this name with Sutol. They are different villages about 8km apart.) Those going to the base camp of Mt. Nandaghunti and southern base camp of Trishul will also pass through Sutol from Ghat. There are no tea houses on this route, though you pass through several villages. The women in this region, as in any other Garhwal village, are fond of jewellery, especially nose and earrings, necklaces and strings of coins. The jewellery is usually passed down the family line, so don't be surprised if you run into someone wearing a string of Victorian coins. The village ladies of Uttarakhand, out of respect, either look down or to the side when a stranger or elder is talking to them. The moment you are in a village, people will start peeping from all directions and in a moment you will be surrounded by men, women and children, all gazing at you in bewilderment.

The last house of the village is about 10 minutes away from the centre and here the route forks. Take the lower 8ft wide mule track behind the house through pine forest. A few short ups and downs and you will reach a bridge over a stream in an hour - a good opportunity to have a wash in the clean water of the stream before your 45 minute climb from here to the village of Peri. The temple at the end of the climb provides a welcome resting place with a cool breeze and is visible from the other side while descending to the bridge. The village is only a few minutes below the path. You continue downward to another small village 20 minutes away, with a tinned roof hut referred to by villagers as the 'Bungalow'. The path to Paltingdhar (2000m), a suggested stop for the night, can be seen from here. Accompanying porters may recommend the tin hut for the night, saying that the water point at Paltingdhar is too far away, but it is advisable to push on a further 3km, taking less than 2 hours, to a beautiful flat campsite on the ridge, a short distance from the village of Paltingdhar. From the tin hut path continue down for half an hour to a stream with a couple of watermills and then uphill for $1\frac{1}{2}$ hours, passing a school below the path. The water point is about 1km short of the village under a grove of oak trees below the main path. It is advisable to fill up with water from here, which will save you a good 25 minutes fetching water after putting up the tents. The view from the camp is superb; in the north-east, Mt. Nandaghunti and Trishul, and south, the expanding Nandakini valley. The village has been set up as a convenient place from which to graze livestock and do seasonal farming.

Day 3: From Paltingdhar the path to the next village, Ala, is very good and almost level except for 10 minutes' uphill. The view of the valley below reveals dotted villages, green forests and terraced fields. Some houses in Ala look very old with carved doors, which used to be very popular over 50 years ago. The path from Ala goes down for 15 minutes to a stream followed by a half-hour uphill walk through forest, ending half a kilometre short of Bura village with lovely shady oak trees for rest and a drinking water tap. The next village, Padergaon, is about 3km on a fairly level path, and 1km beyond is Ramani village which is reached from Ghat in one day, as described earlier. Padergaon is a big village with two shops and a primary school which can be used for accommodation. The teachers, as on all trekking routes, are very helpful. From the school walk for half an hour to Timtha village. From Timtha it is steep uphill into a forest. You must make sure from the villagers that you are on the right track for Jhinji. Although the trail uphill through the forest is reasonably clear there are several goat tracks which can be misleading if you are not careful. A little over half way from Timtha you reach the top of a huge steep rock called Bhaginikhal: across this is a path bearing left to rhododendron forest. Then a steep 10 minute descent takes you to Semkharak (3230m) shepherd huts. There is a nice campsite with a view of Nandaghunti to the north-east, the Badrinath range in the north, the villages of Irani, and to its left to Pana, your next destination across the Birahi Ganga river.

Day 4: A descent to 1600m, taking 3 hours, takes you to the village of Jhinji which has piped water and solar light in the village contractor's house. The entire path is through forest. From Jhinji, the Birahi Ganga appears very close but it takes half an hour down the steep slope and another 15 minutes of level path to reach the 75m high bridge over the Birahi, built during British rule. The school at Jhinji is a good place to spend the night. From here the nearest roadhead is Nijmola, 13km, which connects Chamoli on the Badrinath route with Birahi, 11km. Pana, the last village on the Kwari pass route, is 2 hours uphill from the bridge followed by about an hour's fairly level path through forest with good views of the Birahi Ganga below and distant mountain ranges. A huge landslide far below into the Birahi is clearly visible - it occurred as a result of the breaking up of the large Gauna lake in the mid 70s, causing great havoc and loss of several lives. The lake had caused similar damage in 1893, and is referred to in Shipton's book on Garhwal.

There is an ideal campsite surrounded by huge boulders 1km before the village with several watermills and a stream close by. There are two shops and a two-room guest house at Pana, without toilet facilities. The waterfall close to the camp is spectacular during and after the monsoon.

Day 5: After reaching the village, you commence the uphill journey by taking the upper route above the village. The first climb takes 2 hours. The route alternates through meadow and forest. Then a gradual downhill path for 20 minutes will take you to the shepherd huts of Sartoli Kharak, revealing for the first time a view of the Kwari pass, cutting a notch in the ridge, and snow-covered peaks beyond. This good path goes gently downhill all the way through dense bamboo and rhododendron forest for $1^{1}/_{4}$ hours, then you find yourself standing on top of a very steep craggy hillside, ending at the Pui gadhera stream which appears out of a narrow cleft. This slope is constantly damaged by landslide and large movements of goats. The zigzag trail takes about 15 minutes across the hillside. If you are keeping to schedule, you should be by the stream for lunch and be prepared for a steep uphill walk lasting a little over an hour, through forest. This is called the 'Doma-Bithi' climb. After the climb it is an easy 25 minutes to the Dhakwani stream. Cross the stream and follow the path uphill through forest and meadow for half an hour when you will reach a sloped plateau and across it are two rock overhangs, called the Dhakwani cave (3341m). It is advisable to camp here for the night to enjoy the morning views of the Himalaya.

Day 6: From Dhakwani a fast walker takes $1^{1}/_{2}$ hours to reach the lower Kwari pass and about 40 minutes to return. If you have the steam and inclination you may venture to make a return trip to the lower Kwari pass (4000m) on the evening of Day 5 to climb the 150m ridge to your right above the pass, leaving the path below. It will take about half an hour to reach the ridge for a grand view of the Himalaya, with good light for photography. You must return before it gets dark. This will give you an additional opportunity to enjoy the views and ensure some good photos lest the light is unfavourable the following morning.

From the cave follow the path uphill for 20 minutes, reaching the upper meadow of Dhakwani when the path turns right to the foot of the Kwari pass and marks the end of treeline. It is a zigzag, steep ascent along the gully. This is usually covered with manageable winter snow, right up to mid May in a few places. Occasionally you may notice the path has disappeared due to landslide.

It is advisable to leave Dhakwani early enough to reach the lower Kwari pass by about 8.30am. This is the first viewpoint for the Kedarnath and Badrinath peaks. The Kwari pass proper (4265m) is $1^{1}/_{2}$km further along a gentle, uphill path where you will truly see, in the words of Shipton, "the grandest mountain views in the world". One by one dozens of peaks, including Kedarnath, Chaukhamba, Nilkanth, HathiParbat, GhoriParbat, Dunagiri, Bethartoli, Kamet, Trishul and several others, reveal themselves from north to north-east. On a clear day even peaks in Tibet can be seen, though difficult to identify. Mt. Nandadevi remains in hiding for a couple of hours more. From the pass it is downhill for 10 minutes and then across a few streams and meadows for about 2km when you reach a ridge marked with cairns. From here a clear path goes down to Tapoban, 14km into the Dhauli valley down below, where you can terminate the trek and take a bus to Joshimath. But it is more interesting to continue along the ridge from the cairns to the ski slopes of Auli, about 8km to your left (as you look in the direction of Dhauli valley). The advantage of going along the ridge is you can continue to feast your eyes with the grand mountain panorama and the vast expanse of valley in all directions. The route is easy and enjoyable walking on grass. It goes along the ridge for about 1km, remaining a bit above the treeline, then descends for 10 minutes followed by two or three short ups and downs, when you land in flat meadow by the treeline. The path leads into the forest for about half an hour till you reach a large black muddy pond called Tali, a shepherd's camp.

Now majestic Nandadevi will appear to greet you and feast your eyes till Auli is reached. After passing the muddy pond the main trail goes across the ridge to the Gorson ski slopes, taking about 2 hours. If you have mules or otherwise, a second and more beautiful route is to follow the mule track to the ridge, about 45 minutes' steep uphill but worth the climb. You will need a guide to do this route. There are lovely vast meadows and ridges. In 2 hours you will be in the forest at the end of the Gorson ski slopes. Unfortunately water is scarce in the Gorson meadow and the only possibility for camping is at the end of the meadow below the villagers' summer cowsheds. There is a spring with clean water in the forest and a good place for camping, though there are no mountain views. It is suggested you get up to the ridge early next morning, taking about half an hour, to enjoy a wonderful sunrise on Nandadevi.

Day 7: The path to the ski slopes of Auli goes downhill through the forest. The first landmark is a small temple decorated with colourful bunting. The slopes are considered very good for skiing by international standards. There is a tourist bungalow and other infrastructure for skiing, including a ski lift. Joshimath is 13km by a motorable road from Auli, but a public transport system has not yet been fully developed on this road. There is a ropeway connecting Auli with Joshimath. If you cannot manage a drive, the best thing is to take a 4km footpath straight down to Joshimath from the tea house below the ski resort. Joshimath has a large bazaar to explore, with several cheap lodges. Public transport is also available to several destinations, including the railhead at Rishikesh.

VALLEY OF FLOWERS. GRADE B

Best season: Mid June to end of August when the flowers are in bloom during the monsoon.

The valley became famous from the writings of Frank Smythe. It was in 1931 that Smythe and Holdsworth stumbled into the valley when, at the end of their successful Kamet expedition, they crossed from the village of Ghansali to Bhyundhar pass (5125m) and descended into the valley. Smythe wrote, "The Bhyundhar valley was the most beautiful valley that any of us had seen. We camped in it for two days and we remembered it afterwards as the 'Valley of Flowers'". Legend associates this valley with 'Gandhamadan' and 'Nandankan' from where Hanuman, the monkey god, collected the herb 'Sanjeevani' to revive the badly wounded Laxman, the younger brother of the incarnation god Rama. The valley is 10km long and about 2km wide in a conical shape, with the Pushpawati river flowing through it. The valley has an elevation ranging from 3000 to 4000m. It was designated a National Park about 10 years ago, prohibiting camping, cooking, grazing, etc, so as not to "disturb the environmental conditions and endanger a number of endemic flora". I have reservations, particularly about prohibiting grazing. Ever since grazing has been stopped in the valley you see many fewer flowers as a weed called Polygonum and Balsam Limpetieus

Roylei has overgrown the valley. It has got hold of the ground and pastureland and flowers are permanently ruined. The ground has also been deprived of manure from the droppings of goats and sheep. With the movement of animals during the season, flower seeds used to be automatically buried in the soil. The shepherds used to burn the weed because it was not eaten by the animals. This system not only provided additional manure but also the necessary heat, by fire and exposing the land to sun for a few days, to help germination before the winter snow began. This was the simple law of nature. Compared with the present Valley of Flowers, there are far more flowers in the Kakbhushandi valley, next to Bhyundar, or any other meadow in the Himalaya where hundreds of sheep and goats graze unchecked every day. Be that as it may, flowers start blooming in the valley soon after the snows melt, from June onwards. Maximum flowers are seen during July-August. A flower enthusiast from the UK, Edwina Sasoon, on an organised trek to this valley including Hemkund lake in 1987, identified the following flowers, both on the approach route and in the Valley of Flowers itself:

Clemetis Montana　　　　　*Geranium Pratense*
Nettles　　　　　　　　　　*Balsam-pink and yellow*
Marjoram　　　　　　　　　*Geranium (pink)*
Violets - pale mauve　　　　*Sambucus 'Elderberry'*
Orbanche Cerha　　　　　　*Aquilegia (leaves only)*
Alpine strawberries　　　　*Myositis Sylvatica*
Sorbaria Tomentosa　　　　*Myositis Allpestris*
Polygonum　　　　　　　　*Lindelofia Anchusoides (borage)*
Eucalyptus　　　　　　　　*Kumkum Dhup-Didymocarpus*
Gentiana Lutes (yellow)　　*Primula Denticulata*
Almonds　　　　　　　　　*Sumac*
Hypericum Choisianum　　　*Ipomoea Purpurea*
Rose Webbiana　　　　　　*Verbascum Thepsus*
Japanese Anenomes (white)　*Thespesia Populnea, or Lampas*
Rosa Brunonii　　　　　　　*Hackelia Uncinata*
Berberis Asiatica　　　　　*Pediculories Pyramidata (pink)*
Euphorbia Himalayensis　　*Morina Longifolia*
Arisaema Tortuosa　　　　　*Viola Wallichiana*
Oxalis Corniculate　　　　　*Meconopsis latifolia*
Arisaema Nepenthoides　　　*Geum Elatum*
Oxalis Latifolia　　　　　　*Yellow Potentilla*
Roscoae Purpurea　　　　　*Primula Wigramiana*
Datura Stramonium　　　　　*Androsace Primuloides*

Iris Kemaonsis
Buttercup
Dectylorhiza Hatagirea (orchid)
Campanula Aristata
Cypripedium Himalaicum
Willow Herb
Anaphalis Triplinervis
    (everlasting)
Sile Edgeworthii
Aconitum Spicatum (Monk's
    Hood)
Astilbe Rivularis
Fritilleraries (green and blue)
Primula Maacrophylla
Lillium Oxypetalum
Heather
Saussurea Obvallata

(Brahmakamal)
Rhododendron (cream)
Corydalis Cashimirianai
Bergenia
Potentilla Cinquefoil
Anemone tetrasepala
Spiraea Arcuata
Parochaetus
Rhodiola Wallichiana (sedum)
Lily of the valley
Ribes
Rhododendron (dwarf yellow)
Ranunculus Hirtellus (marsh
    Marigolds)
Poligonatum Multiflorum
    (Solomon seal)

Approach Route: It is advisable to spend the night at Joshimath and take the first 'gate' (departure of vehicles) leaving at 6.30am for Badrinath. It takes about an hour to reach Govindghat (1829m), the beginning of a 14km trek to Ghangharia, base for the Valley of Flowers and Hemkunt lake. The road is metalled for 1km up to the bridge on Alaknanda. Govindghat bustles with the activities of travellers and pilgrims for it is also the route for the Sikh shrine Hemkunt. It is believed that Guru Govind Singh, the tenth Guru of the Sikh faith, meditated on the bank of Hemkunt lake in his previous life. There is a gurudwara (Sikh shrine) and Lakshman temple on the banks of the lake. It has become a place of pilgrimage for both Sikh and Hindu communities. There is a gurudwara at Govindghat and one at Ghangharia. Accommodation and meals are offered in gurudwaras to anyone, irrespective of religious faith. Before entering a gurudwara cover your head, take off your shoes and do not smoke anywhere near it.

Several eating places, shops, a police station, Post Office and a porter agency all crowded together in a small space make it an interesting place. The porters here are mostly Nepalese. They carry 35 to 40kg. You can hand over your baggage to porters with instructions as to where to find you in Ghangharia, usually the tourist bungalow or the gurudwara, and depart at your own pace. Porters will arrive at your destination 2-3 hours after you. Don't leave things like warm jackets, which you will need immediately on arrival, with the porters.

There is only one path across the bridge. You can safely assume that anyone going uphill is heading for Ghangharia. The whole path is well maintained and zigzaged to ease the steep gradient. Almost every 2-3km there are tea houses serving simple meals, snacks and soft drinks cooled in a bucket of water! The first village you pass is Pulna, 3km, on the right bank of the Hemganga, named after its source Hemkunt. The village of Bhyundhar is 7km from Pulna at 2239m. From here the main path continues to Ghangharia, and east, across a stream, is a shepherd's trail to Kakbhushandi lake (4325m), 18km across the Kankulkhal pass (4630m). It is a very beautiful area for flowers, a mountain panorama of Hathi Parbat, Ghori Parbat and the peaks of the Nandadevi Sanctuary. Kakbhushandi can be reached in 3 days from Govindghat by a self-sufficient party. Make the first day's camp about 6km beyond Bhyundar and 1km from Rupdhungi. The second day reach Rajkharak (3785m), about 3km beyond Dangkharak, and the third day Kakbhushandi lake. Ghangharia is a bit disappointing, a wet place in the middle of deodar forest. During the season it is difficult to find accommodation here. The tourist bungalow, gurudwara and two simple lodges are always packed with visitors, and there is no suitable campsite. A tent site near the helipad, about 15 minutes' walk before Ghangaria, does not have running water. For meals there are several eating places. The small hamlet becomes quite colourful by evening, when hundreds of travellers are around, exchanging information, posing for photographs, singing, dancing or simply sipping tea. A visit to the gurudwara is an extraordinary experience. Everyone is very well received in a gurudwara. The Sikhs perform 'Kar Seva' (community service to mankind) in gurudwaras. Every Sikh will do some free service such as cooking, serving food, cleaning the rooms, cleaning pilgrims' shoes or attending to any repairs when he is on a pilgrimage. Those visiting the gurudwara are given 'Karha Prasad' (semolina) to eat as a blessing at the end of prayers. It is customary to accept it with reverence, keeping the right palm over the left.

From Ghangharia it is 4km to the Valley of Flowers. A little beyond the first bridge the route forks; the one to your right is to Hemkunt, take the left fork for the Valley of Flowers. It rises gradually for about half an hour followed by 10 minutes' descent to the bridge on the Pushpawati river. In August there are blue poppies on this latter stretch. At the bridge you will be met by the National Park wardens who will charge a fee and issue a receipt valid for 3 days to visit the valley. Animals are not permitted beyond this point.

It is a zigzag ascent with rocky slopes on the left bank of the river

Trader

and a dense forest on the right bank for about 1km, when the gorge widens, the trees, mostly silver birch, start thinning out and flowers begin to show.

The main path to the Valley of Flowers is on the west of the Pushpawati river, but the eastern side is more beautiful. It can be reached until the end of July via a snow bridge over the Pushpawati, about 2km from the bridge. There is a shelf about 3km long and $^1/_2$km wide with birch and rhododendron forest above and below. A walk across this shelf, with gentle gradient, provides a fabulous sight with Mt. Rataban (6130m) dominating the scene across the valley. From the upper plateau there is a trail going down through a gully lined with birch and rhododendron bushes to the river. Here there is a snow bridge until about the first week of August over the river. From the snow bridge you can see the Bhyundhar pass crossed by Smythe. Keep to the path on the right bank of the river to get back to Ghangharia. A day return trip to the Valley of Flowers takes about 8 hours.

HEMKUNT LAKE (4328m). GRADE B

Hemkunt is also called Lokpal. It is a beautiful lake encircled by seven snow-clad peaks of around 5000-6000m. The peaks reflect beautifully in the clear water of the lake. There is a big gurudwara on which extension work has been going on for several years. It is made of concrete and steel with a tin roof. Huge iron bars, girders, machines, steel frames, cement, etc, are carried all the way from Govindghat to Hemkund for 20km on the backs of mules and porters. It is an incredible operation, carried out with a lot of imagination and improvisation. Very heavy machines are dismantled at Govindghat and carried in smaller sections, hoisted on logs lifted by four to eight strong porters plus the same number in reserve. They are reassembled at Hemkunt. The building is a fine example of dedicated professional workmanship. It is designed to withstand storms and heavy snowfall during the four winter months. Everyone visiting the gurudwara is offered a free glass of steaming tea by the 'Sewadars' (workers). Devotees take a dip in the freezing cold water of the lake before attending prayers in the main hall.

Hemkunt is 6km uphill from Ghangharia, the first 3km through forest. It takes $4^{1}/_{2}$ hours to walk up and 2 hours back downhill. Riding ponies are available for hire. There are tea houses and eating places on the way. The Public Works Department does regular road maintenance to keep open a safe path through the avalanched snow fields in June, with a rope for hand support. One and a half kilometres short of Hemkunt, about a thousand concrete steps have been built up to the lake. Instead of climbing the steps it is less tiring to walk along the zigzag path. On both sides of the path blue poppies and Brahma kamal (Saussurea Ovallata), a strongly perfumed flower, are in bloom during July-August. The Brahma kamal, the lotus of the god Brahma, is offered at temples. It is more convenient to walk down the steps on the return journey.

GANGOTRI-GAUMUKH (3892m). GRADE C

This trek starts from Gangotri and goes past the snout of the Gangotri glacier at Gaumukh, 18km, where the legendary Bhagirathi river, more commonly known as the holy Ganga, emerges. The scenery is extraordinarily beautiful, with snow-capped peaks soaring above. Tapoban, about 4 hours' trek from Gaumukh, is a spectacular alpine meadow situated nearly at the foot of Mt. Shivling. It is also the base camp for Mt. Karchakkund, Kedarnath, Meru and Bhartekunta.

Season: End of April to mid November. The monsoon months of July-August are very good for alpine flowers. There will be snow beyond Chirbas until about mid May but it is not difficult to find the path.

Approach: The trek commences at Gangotri, details of which are given under Temples of Garhwal.

Day 1: From Gangotri take the path behind the temple. Several hundred years ago the Gangotri glacier extended to here but over the period has receded to its present position. Beautiful deodar, blue pine and juniper line the path all the way to Chirbas (3516m), 9km, with beautiful falls and the snow-covered peaks of Matri, Chirbas and Mandha above and the Bhagirathi river flowing below. Mt. Bhagirathi appears as you approach Chirbas. The well-maintained path is fairly level and the climb is not strenuous. It takes 4 hours to reach Chirbas, which has several eating places during the season. The campsite by the Bhagirathi is just 5 minutes downhill from the tea houses. Those not acclimatised well are advised to camp here overnight and do Gaumukh and back from this camp next morning. A fit person could continue another 5km to Bhojbas, taking about 3 hours. A magnificent Mandha and Shivling appear before you as you walk amongst the rhododendron forest, which starts dwindling and disappears altogether after about 3km. The valley above Chirbas opens up and becomes much grander, with a more rugged appearance.

Day 2: About 2km from Chirbas, where you cross the bridge, if you climb the ridge 200m straight up the path, a glorious view of Bhagirathi, Kharchkund and Mt. Shivling is displayed in triangular fashion. From here, rather than walking back to the path you left, you can continue across the huge flat meadow for about half a kilometre and then take the gentle downhill slope to join the main path near Bhojbas. Between Chirbas and Bhojbas be on the lookout for burrhels (blue mountain sheep) just above and below the path.

There is a tourist bungalow and the Ashram of a sadhu, who is pleased to offer accommodation at Bhojbas (3792m). There is also a nice camping place by the river.

Day 3: In early May there is usually a snow bridge on the Bhagirathi about 15 minutes' walk from Bhojbas, along the right bank of the river, which is convenient for reaching Tapoban and avoiding the moraine. However, the snow bridge cannot be relied upon, so the usual route is to follow the path to the source of the Ganges, or Gaumukh, 4km, then walk across the glacier. The views of the Gangotri glacier and the peaks surrounding it, the vast granite rockface with the snow-covered tops of the three Bhagirathis, and the beautiful Shivling towering aloft are truly impressive. Suddenly you find yourself at Gaumukh (cow's snout) with huge blue ice walls under which the Bhagirathi gushes out of the glacier. You will notice Hindu devotees praying by the river. It takes 2 hours from Bhojbas to the source of the Ganges. From here Tapoban is a further 3 hours. The path is about 200m above the snout going north-east across the glacier towards Shivling. It is a typical huge rubble desert, pitted with crevasses and studded with snowmelt emerald pools. Under the rubble are several feet of deep blue ice. Crossing this glacier is no different from crossing any other glacier in the Himalaya: it is time-consuming and frustrating. The local porters are familiar with the route and are very helpful. It takes $1^{1}/_{2}$ hours to reach the saddle over a steep slope up the moraine, punctuated by huge boulders. From this saddle you turn north-west along an easy trail with mainly grassy slopes above and the glacier below. The beautiful Shivling has by this time come into view again. The panorama now ahead is absolutely stunning. The Bhagirathis, Sudarshan, Matri, Srikailash, the huge snowy bulk of Kharchakund, Shivling and several other peaks above 6000m tower above the vast expanse of the glacier. A short steep walk up a ridge brings you to Tapoban, a meadow about half a kilometre wide and 2km long, a perfect campsite with glacial streams flowing through it. You can spend an enjoyable two or three days using this as a base camp for day return trips, including Nandanban, the base camp of Bhagirathi just 2km across the glacier. From Nandanban the route also goes to Badrinath, across the Kalindikhal pass in 6 days, but no one is permitted to do this route without special permission from the District Magistrates of Uttarkashi and Chamoli both.

* * *

On the return journey you can easily make Chirbas in 5 hours and Gangotri in another 3 hours. From Gangotri you can reach Kedartal lake (4701m) along the Kedarganga in two days to enjoy close views of the Jogin group of peaks, the highest being 6465m. The path goes above the PWD rest house across Bhagirathi and is steep uphill all the way. The second and better short trek from Gangotri is to Rudugaira Bamak along the ridge of the Patangnidhar. It is a much wider and more interesting valley than the Kedarganga valley. Rudugaira Bamak can be reached in 2 days. It provides close-up views of the Gangotri group of peaks (highest 6672m), Jaonli group (6632m), Srikantha (6133m), and Rudugaira (5819m). You will need a guide to do these routes and must be self-sufficient.

GANGOTRI-KEDARNATH TREK. GRADE C
Season: May to mid November.
This is an old pilgrimage route which is no longer used by pilgrims, who make use of the convenient motorways to save both time and effort. This is, however, a delightful trek through beautiful landscape, dense forest, large high-altitude meadows and grand mountain views. You trek across the Kush Kalyan range and Panwali meadows to Kedarnath. There are no technical difficulties on the way. The path is reasonably clear throughout and additional guidance can be had from villagers and shepherds. Tents must be carried on this route.
Approach route: From Gangotri drive down to Lata (1478m) to commence the trek. Lata is a small village 4km beyond Bhatwari

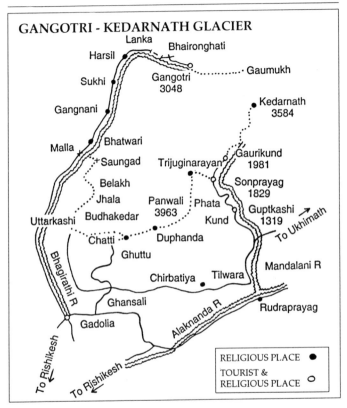

GANGOTRI - KEDARNATH GLACIER

RELIGIOUS PLACE ●

TOURIST & RELIGIOUS PLACE ○

where you should purchase provisions and vegetables for two days. Some advise stopping at Malla which is 2km beyond Bhatwari, and walking down the road across the bridge. But Lata is more convenient for the night as there are a few tea houses with one or two rooms. Alternatively there is a small camping place across the bridge. It is advisable to leave Gangotri in the afternoon, spend the night at Lata and leave early next morning. Those coming from Rishikesh to do this portion of the trek are advised to spend the night at Uttarkashi, arrange porters, provisions, etc. and drive early next morning, taking about an hour to reach Lata.

Day 1: From Lata village walk down to the bridge on Bhagirathi and follow the path on the left bank, gradually ascending to the village of Saura reached in half an hour. After crossing the village continue on the upper path through pine forest for another 2km to the Dogadda river. It takes 2 hours to reach the cowsheds by the river from Lata. From now on it is all the way uphill through forests of oak, rhododendron and pine to Belakh (2439m) taking 4 hours. Midway to Belakh from the river Dogadda, Chhunna is a deserted shepherds' camp and stopping-off place for pilgrims in the old days. Belakh, with a few tea houses in thatched huts, provides a first view of the snow-clad peaks in the Bunderpunch range. These tea houses also cater for simple meals and provide community floor accommodation on one side of their smoky rooms. Nearby is a campsite for 4-5 tents.

Those interested in starting the trek from Uttarkashi can take a bus to Chaurangikhal, 9km, across Bhagirathi and commence the walk through forests and ridges via Kamand. This provides better views and takes 2 days to reach Belakh. A guide is recommended on this path.

If you do not wish to spend the night at Belakh, there is a nice campsite about 45 minutes' downhill walk towards Budhakedar in the forest by the side of a spring at about 1850m. Next day it is about 2 hours downhill to Jhala chatti (1749m).

* * *

Extension Option

From Belakh there is a very interesting side trip to Kushkalyan (3836m), Okryatal lake (approximately 4200m) and several other lakes in the region. It is a shepherds' path heading east through forest and you would need either a guide or some clear directions from people at Belakh.

The first hour is uphill till you reach the first vast meadow. Later it is a gentle uphill and a few short descents. Jorai, also known as Dana Kharak, will take about 3 hours. The villagers' cowsheds are rather low and dirty. They keep their cows on one side with an entrance door, with about 4 x 6ft of sleeping area and a fireplace on the other side, with a separate entrance. The entrance doors are very low; you have to bend considerably to get into the hut. The Gujjars (Nomads) build a much better pyramid shaped hut with a large hall, a fireplace in the middle and partitioned cubicles without doors for sleeping around the fireplace. Young calves are kept together in one cubicle for protection from the cold; other animals remain outside the hut during the night. You need to watch out for fierce shepherds' dogs, particularly during the night. They are usually not harmful during the day unless provoked or surprised.

From Jorai the trail continues across alternating meadows and forests to Mati Kharak, cowsheds belonging to the villagers of Pinswar, for the overnight camp, reached in about 3 hours. The highlights of the trek are the views of surrounding meadows and of the Bandarpunch peaks. Mati, at about 3250m, has a lovely campsite in the middle of forest with water close by. It is an ideal base from which to make a day return trip to Kushkalyan. Leave early to reach the top in 2 hours and view the peaks in their full glory. Kushkalyan is not a peak but the highest point of the meadow and easy to get to. The views of wide meadow and the mountain panoramas of Bandarpunch, Gangotri, Kedarnath and Badrinath peaks are superb. Many Monal pheasants may also be seen en route. You can spend the whole day sitting there on soft turf under the bright sun simply doing nothing but admiring the stupendous views and thinking what a wonderful atom of the world you are in.

From Mati you can return to the motorway at Malla, 16km, on the way to Uttarkashi via Sila village, midway. There is a rest house at Sila. The path is mostly downhill and passes through the cowsheds of Gautu. It will take one day from Mati to walk down to Jhala chatti via Pinswar village to continue on the Kedarnath trek via Budhakedar (second day's stage from Belakh, described below).

If you have time and a guide an extension to Lamtalu, Okryatal and Sahastratal lakes would be rewarding. The route from Mati is to Bawani in one day. You will need to retrace your steps to the highest point of the trail done on the approach route from Belakh and then head eastward along the ridges. Next day will take you to Kyarki huts or Patlikharak nearby at abut 3450m. The trail is across ridges, forests and meadows with excellent views and plenty of high-altitude birds.

It is possible from Patlikharak to make a return trip to Lamtalu lake, Kukli tal lake and Okryatal lake in about 10 hours. All the lakes are extremely well situated. The waters of Okryatal are particularly pleasant-tasting. A guide is a must on this extension. From Patlikharak it is mostly uphill along a ridge to the first lake, Lamtalu, which takes about an hour. In another hour you will be at Kuklital. Now the downhill path is through Kuklia danda for 45 minutes, ending at Dogargad stream. It is gentle uphill along a ridge for about $1^{1}/2$ hours to Okryatal. Many Monal and snow pheasants can be seen in this region and with a bit of luck some wildlife such as musk deer and blue mountain sheep (Burrhel). This is virtually an unexplored area and a superb place to visit. There are three more lakes in the region: Matrytal (also known as Parikatal or Fairy's lake), Narsingha tal and

. . .grand mountain panoramas and lovely meadows. . . Photo: John Martin

Sahastru tal, all of which can be reached almost within a day from Okryatal. Nowhere else in the Himalaya will you find so many beautiful lakes, grand mountain panoramas and lovely meadows as in this region. The return journey should be via Pinswar village, which can be reached in one day via Kushkalyan. This extension will take a total of 4 days, ending at Pinswar.

* * *

Day 2: Jhala is a small village across the Dharam Ganga, downhill all the way from Belakh via forest. A few tea houses and watermills provide a good excuse to rest. This place is well known for the local bamboo mats, used by villagers to dry grain. From here onwards there is a nice mule track across the bridge on the Dharam Ganga. The path is along its left bank with tempting pools for bathing. It is a gentle walk with terraced fields and villages on both sides. The entire route is also very good for birdwatching. The river is full of trout so if you are carrying a fishing rod, you will not have to be patient for long. The biggest village in the valley, Thati Kathur, is also called Budhakedar (1542m). It is 6km away taking about 2$^{1}/_{2}$ hours from Jhala. Budhakedar has a few shops to replenish your supplies, some eating places, and a PWD bungalow about 150m above the bridge after the village. If the bungalow is not free, there is a school which may be approached for

accommodation or to put up tents on a flat patch nearby. It is advisable to enquire about the keeper of the bungalow from the tea house across the bridge before starting the climb to the bungalow. Budhakedar is also a bus terminus with connections to Ghansali and Tehri.

Day 3: From Budhkedar, Bhairon Chatti is 10km taking about 5 hours. The path goes above the bungalow for an hour through pine forest all the way up to Binakkhal village, with shops, school and a connecting road. It has good views of the valley below. Walk along the road for 300m and take the upper path through terraced fields and villages to the next landmark, the big village of Bheti. A few ups and downs and you are at Tula hamlets by the side of a stream at about 1640m. A 6ft wide path through silver oak forest and several villages is well made. There are a couple of tea houses on the way. It is now all the way up again through forest, gradually revealing the mountain views. Bhairon Chatti (2493m) is a seasonal village with thatched houses in the middle of forest to facilitate cattle grazing. There is a temple dedicated to the god Bhairon and a huge flat area, making it an ideal camping place. A bit of Kedarnath range is visible. Water is scarce here but it is worth spending a free afternoon. During the season it is possible to buy fresh milk in the village.

Day 4: Ghuttu (1630m) is 13km away. The path is a mixture of flat, a few short uphills and then mostly downhill via some shepherds' huts. Near Bhatgaon, at Kopardhar, is a big state-run angora rabbit and sheep breeding farm with a commanding view of the surroundings and the Bhilangna valley. From here it is an hour's downhill walk through the village of Janali, ending at the road to Ghuttu from Ghansali and Rishikesh via Tehri. The last 4km is on the road with tea houses on the way. Ghuttu is a big village on both sides of the Bhilangna river. It has a big market with eating places, fresh provisions, etc. and is the takeoff point for Khatling glacier via Gangi village. Details are given separately. There is a tourist bungalow at Ghuttu but no proper campsite.

Instead of spending the night at Ghuttu, it is recommended to continue 4km further to Pyau Kharak, about 2$^{1}/_{2}$ hours uphill, though water is scarce and far off at Pyau. Alternatively, camp by the watermill at Gawanagad stream, with space for two or three tents, taking an hour from Ghuttu. The cool water of the stream is very refreshing.

Day 5: It is 9km to Panwali (3433m) from Pyau Kharak, taking about 6 hours. Fifteen minutes after leaving Pyau Kharak there is a shortcut straight uphill through dense forest, taking about an hour, to Gawan Manda Kharak, while the longer main mule track takes a zigzag path. There are a few cowsheds here and a water spring. The uphill path through silver oak and rhododendron forest continues for an hour more till a hut is reached on the ridge and the first snow-covered mountain views of the Gangotri range appear. The next half-hour is fairly level then there is a quarter of an hour uphill and then flat again for about 1km. The valley becomes wider and more beautiful. Lush green meadows appear one after the other. The final climb to the col of Panwali takes 25 minutes, with a lovely panorama of the Garhwal Himalaya. From the col it takes a further 20 minutes downhill to the camp and hamlets of Panwali amidst wide meadow surrounded by forests. There is a Dharamshala here. The most suitable campsite is by the side of a dilapidated rest house close by, with the slight disadvantage that water is about 12 minutes' walk past the Dharamshala. During the season villagers set up a few tea houses here. Fresh milk, simple cooked meals, potatoes, rice, wheat flour, salt and occasional sugar can be purchased. Panwali is one of the most beautiful meadows in Uttarakhand with fabulous views of almost the entire Garhwal Himalaya to over 300km, including the highest peak, Nandadevi. The views of sunset and sunrise are unforgettable. In May, sunrise on the mountains is at about 5.20am and by 5.40am the tents are lit with sunshine. The meadows are spread out for several miles, and in summer thousands of sheep and goats will be grazing on them. Some of the shepherds come all the way from Himachal Pradesh. They spin the wool to make into large balls which are carried home for weaving during the winter. Some carry shawls and light blankets with them for sale to the villagers they pass by on the several days long journey to get to the high pasture. These items, in natural colours, are well made, warm, and cost much less than in the market. Occasionally you may also be able to watch the rather cruel method of shearing the sheep, with crude scissors and even sickles! An extra day spent here will not go without its reward. The meadows will be covered with flowers in season.

Day 6: It is possible to reach Trijuginarayan, 12km, in one day in about 8 hours. The first part of the route, about 4km, is mostly along the ridge. The village of Gangi can be seen after a while on the right bank of the Bhilangna river. There are mountain panoramas galore. Before getting to Kyonkholakhal it is half an hour's steep downhill followed by half an hour uphill. From there you continue downhill, passing through a dilapidated hamlet called Maggu. Views of Kedarnath and Chaukhamba peaks can be had from the lower slopes. Maggu used to be a popular stopping-off place in the old pilgrimage days, but no one stops here now. Continue the downward journey right up to Trijuginarayan (1942m). The path is clear. There are dharamshalas and tea houses for accommodation but there is no place for camping. Those who prefer camping should do so on a lovely flat ground about 2km short of Trijuginarayan where the main forest ends. From the village you can either walk down to Sonprayag, 3km, or take a bus ride to Gaurikund via Sonprayag, 5km, and continue the trek to Kedarnath, as explained under 'Temples'.

KHATLING GLACIER (3717m). GRADE C+

Season: May-June and September-October. Khatling glacier was formed by the chain of mountains around it, namely the Jaonli group (6632m), Jogin group (6465m), Phating, also called Thalai Sagar (6904m), Kirti Stambh (6270m) and Bhartekunta (6578m). From the glacier there are stunning views of all these peaks. Phating looks dazzling with its steep crystal quartz face. It is the source of the Bhilangna river on which the largest dam in Asia is being built, at Tehri. According to legend a celestial Bhil girl tried to lure Lord Shiva while he was meditating. In anger, Shiva pushed her in the river. It has thus been called Bhilangna (Bhil + Ang, meaning body). The trek passes through thick forest and, higher up, lush green meadow. It is rich in wildlife, particularly black bears, and is adorned by delightful waterfalls and lakes. Many a stream has to be crossed on this trek so it is not recommended during the monsoon, despite the great temptation of alpine flowers in profusion. Tents and provisions must be carried.

Approach route: The trek starts from Ghuttu, the bus terminus. Ghuttu is connected by bus to Rishikesh, via Tehri and Ghansali, 35km. Buses also ply between Tehri and Ghuttu, 66km, twice a day.

Day 1: Reeh village (2132m), partly through forest, takes 5 hours from Ghuttu. Take the lefthand broad path gently uphill from the bus terminus along the right bank of the Bhilangna.

There is a tourist bungalow at Reeh below the village with just enough space for two tents by the side of the bungalow. The village

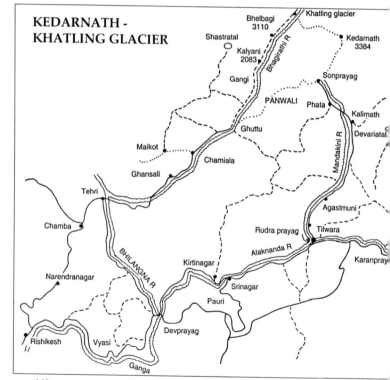

KEDARNATH - KHATLING GLACIER

is high above the path and cannot be counted on for accommodation.

Day 2: Gangi (2584m), the last village en route, takes 5 hours. The first 2 hours on a clear path is steeply uphill, about 600m climb, followed by gradual downhill, ending up with fairly level path. The scenery is splendid, with views of Panwali across the Bhilangna, dense forests of oak, walnuts and rhododendron and some towering waterfalls. The village school, with space for two tents, and a tourist bungalow can be used for the night. Gangi commands a panoramic view of the valley. Further north the snow-covered Himalaya appear on the skyline. Gangi gets cut off from the market centre of Ghuttu and other villages in winter due to snow and landslides. The village seems to have remained uninfluenced by the developments in the rest of Garhwal. They follow age old customs passed down the generations. Marriage is always from within the community and the groom has to pay several thousand rupees, occasionally as many as twenty thousand, for the bride. It is therefore important for them to save money for their marriage from the sale of potatoes and beans, grown in large quantities. Inbreeding coupled with genital infection has been responsible for the gradual decline of the village population which currently stands at less than 400. People of the village look alike and rather different from other Garhwalis. Their other means of livelihood is sheep breeding. Each family has its own flock of sheep, and during summer all the sheep are sent to Bugyals under the care of a few people paid to stay and look after them for the season. The villagers take turns to supply them with provisions. Most of the wool is used to make clothes for their own needs and the surplus is sold to tradesmen. This practice of rearing goats and sheep in Bugyals is adopted all over Uttarakhand.

Day 3: From Gangi it is a lovely 3 hours' walk to Kalyani shepherd camp via dense forest. From Kalyani most people go to Bhelbagi for the night, though I do not recommend the steep slopes of Bhelbagi for camping. There is a lovely campsite at Kharsoli (2896m) shepherd camp, 2km short of Bhelbagi, beside a stream in the middle of forest. And there is a large Gujjar hut which is unoccupied from October to May and can be used. The whole area provides a beautiful setting.

Day 4: It takes only half an hour to get to Bhelbagi from Kharsoli along an easy path.

* * *

A further half-hour beyond the cave of Bhumka is a bridge on the Bhilangna which has to be crossed if you want to make a 4 day trek to Kedarnath. After crossing the bridge follow the goat track on the left side of the river up to the Khatling glacier then turn on to the left bank of the Dudh Ganga river. Remember that it is not possible to cross the Bhilangna at Khatling. Following the Dudh Ganga bamak, Masartal lake (3675m), about 6km, takes 5 hours. It is worthwhile to camp by the lake before commencing the ascent next day. It is important to have a guide on this trek to Kedarnath as the walk is rather strenuous on one day through glacier, loose boulders and steep rocky terrain. Maximum height reached would be about 4800m. Six kilometres short of Kedarnath, the beautiful lake of Vasukital is surrounded by pretty meadows studded with flowers in summer. From here it is downhill to the temple.

* * *

To go to Khatling glacier continue on the clear trail from Bhumka bridge on the right bank of the Bhilangna. It is steep uphill all the way. As you go higher the mountains start to appear in their full glory. There is no suitable campsite at the glacier. The day return journey from Kharsoli, with an hour at the glacier, will take about 9 hours. An early start is recommended.

Wood carved house. Photo: Anup Shah

Western Garhwal

DODITAL LAKE TREK (3307m). GRADE B

Season: End of March to mid June, and October to end of November. Located in the middle of dense forest consisting mainly of oak, deodar, rhododendron and thin bamboo (Ringal), Dodital Lake is a little over 1km in circumference. It is famous for Himalayan trout. Permits for fishing can be had from the Divisional Forest Officer, Uttarkashi. The region is rich in bird and wildlife. During the summer season Gujjar nomads can be seen camping with their herds of buffalo. They are very friendly and hospitable people. You can also enter the Yamnotri valley at Hanuman chatti from Dodital. Meals are available on the way and a guide is not needed.

Approach route: The base for this trek is Uttarkashi where porters can be arranged and provisions bought. From Uttarkashi there is a regular bus service twice a day to Kalyani, and Sangam chatti (1829m), 13km. A jeep taxi can also be hired at any time. The drive for the first 4km up to Gangori is on the Gangotri route. From Gangori it turns north-west along the left bank of the Kaldigad through pine forest. There are several beautiful campsites along the driving route on the river bank.

The trek starts from Sangam chatti across the river on a gradual uphill path through forest, terraced fields and Agora village. It is advisable to spend the first night at Baibra, 7km (2280m), with plenty of camping places by a stream and two tea houses serving simple meals. This place is about 20 minutes' walk from Agora. There is a two-room forest bungalow and a private guest house at Agora with eating facilities.

The next day's trek to Dodital is 14km through attractive forest, taking about 7 hours. It is a well-made mule track with views of Dayara top with excellent ski slopes. There are several campsites by the lake and eating places at Dodital, with dormitory type accommodation. You must, however, carry a sleeping bag. The dilapidated forest bungalow is unsafe to spend the night. You can spend two or three fascinating days at Dodital for short day return treks. For excellent views of the Bandarpunch (6387m) and Kalanag peaks, a day return trip taking about 6 hours to Kansara pass (3962m) is recommended. It is a fascinating route, going for about an hour along the stream feeding the lake. The stream has to be crossed and recrossed about 8 times, but the entire route is reasonably clear. If you have another 3 days at your disposal you can reach Hanuman Chatti for Yamunotri. This route is mostly downhill from the Kansara pass on the Darwa ridge. There are Gujjar huts for overnight shelter on the way. The Byakula Gad and Mundrala streams are crossed to enter Kothi meadow through rhododendron and conifer forest. The first village reached in the Hanuman Ganga valley is Nishni followed by Hanuman Chatti with a tourist bungalow, some guest houses and several eating places. From there transport is available for Mussoorie, Dehra Dun or Rishikesh.

Deviations from Uttarkashi

1. DAYARA TREK. GRADE B
This is an all-season, very enjoyable short trek to the Dayara meadows (3635m) with great panoramic views of the Bandarpunch, Gangotri and Kushkalyan ranges. Dayara slopes have great potential for a ski resort.

Approach: Drive to Barsu village, 37km from Uttarkashi via Bhatwari, 25km. Barsu (1990m) is a big prosperous village where accommodation and any other help can be arranged through Jagmohan Singh Rawat, a very cooperative senior official of the village development committee. If you need them, porters should be arranged from Uttarkashi.

Dayara meadows are only about 8km from Barsu on a mule track through forest. You can conveniently make a day return trip from Barsu in about 8-9 hours. It would, however, be more satisfying to spend a night at Dayara, either camping if you carry a tent or in the shepherd huts. The views on the way up and from the meadow cover Banderpunch, Kalanag, Jaonali, Srikanth, Dropadi Ka Danda and Kushkalyan. Even a leisurely walk through the meadow which spreads for several miles is worth spending an extra day.

From Dayara you can also reach Dodital in 2 days along the ridge and through forest rich in bird and wildlife. The region is particularly known for the beautiful Monal pheasant. A guide and tents will be needed for the Dodital section.

2. SUKHI - HANUMAN CHATTI VIA BAMSARUKHAL (4786m). GRADE C/D
Season: June to October.
This is a fascinating but strenuous high-altitude trek through forest and meadow. Participants must be self-sufficient with tents, provisions and a guide from Uttarkashi. Grand panoramas of the Gangotri, Bandarpunch and Swargrohini ranges and peaks of Himachal can be

had from several places.

Approach route: The trek starts from Sukhi (2744m) about 3 hours' drive from Uttarkashi in the direction of Gangotri. It takes 6 days to complete this trek. The goat path is above the village leading to the Chaingad stream. There is a good campsite about 2 hours' walk from Sukhi. Following the left bank of the Chaingad, Bamsarukhal pass (4786m), Kanatal and Sonpara ridge you will reach Hanuman Chatti. Please note that the author does not have personal experience of this trek; this scant information was collected from local shepherds.

HARKIDOON (3030m). GRADE B

Best season: Mid April to June and mid September to end of November. The Tons valley, formed by the rivers Rupin and Supin, is amongst the first regions to be discovered by British explorers early this century. During 1940-50 Jim Gibbson, Jak Martin and R.L. Holdsworth, illustrious headmasters of Doon School, Dehra Dun, popularised the Harkidoon meadows in a big way for Indian and foreign students studying in India. Soon it came to be known as one of the most beautiful Himalayan regions, easily accessible. From May onwards, like elsewhere, flowers start blooming in the meadows. June, July and August give a fabulous combination of colours. You do, however, have to be mentally attuned and equipped to brave the monsoon to enjoy the flowers. There are lakes, beautiful meadows and close-up panoramic views of the Swargarohini, Kalanag and Bandarpunch group of peaks. The Rupin river originates from the borders of Himachal Pradesh and the Uttarkashi district of Uttar Pradesh. Supin originates from the Kimla pass. Both these rivers join at Naitwar. It is then called the Tons - another casualty of British pronunciation. Its original name is Tamsha. It merges with the Yamuna at Kalsi about 40km from Dehra Dun. People from Tons valley practise very different social and religious customs. For example, they worship Druyodhana, chief of the evil force in the epic *Mahabharata* in which Krishna, the incarnation god, was on the side of the opposite force, Pandavas. At Naitwar there is a temple to the local deity Pokhu, which you must enter by keeping your back to the deity with hands folded. It is believed that if you face it, misfortune will come to you, and you worship the deity by keeping your back to it to seek protection and blessings. Some people still practise polyandry in this region. They are very fond of singing and dancing. Women have very pretty sharp features. Some of their houses look like pagodas. The path being obvious, a guide is not needed on this trek.

Approach route: Approach to this valley is from Dehra Dun to

HARKIDOON TREK

Borasu Pass 5360

Osla 2569 · · · Harkidoon 3586

Taluka

Netwar 1401

Mori

To Yamunotri

Jarmola

Purola

BARKOT 2118

Lakhamandal

Naogaon 1372

TO CHAKRATA

YAMUNA

Kuwa

TO CHAKRATA

TO CHAKRATA

KEMPTY FALLS

Yamuna bridge

Dakpathar

Kalsi

HERBERTPUR

TO HARDWAR /RISHIKESH

TO SAHARANPUR

Dehra Dun

TO DELHI

RELIGIOUS PLACE	O
TOURIST PLACE	+
TOURIST & RELIGIOUS PLACE	●

Sankri, 195km. A public bus leaves Dehra Dun, near the railway station, at around 6am and reaches Sankri by 5pm. Taxis can also be hired and would take 7 hours. The road is via Mussoorie and Naugaon, 105km, on the Yamnotri route. Before Naugaon there is a very interesting old village, Lakhamandal, dating back to the 5th century BC and the Mahabharata period. To get to this village you alight at Kunwa. Lakhamandal is across the Yamuna. You can drive very close to the village. According to legends, it was here that the Kauravas of the epic *Mahabharata* built the Laksha Griha (Shellac

174

Palace) to lure the Pandavas, their cousins, into gambling and to burn them alive. But the Pandavas escaped with their consort Dropadi from the Shellac Palace through a narrow underground passage, which leads to the Yamuna river. This passage still exists and can be seen. The villagers call themselves descendants of the Pandavas and hold an annual fair in the memory of King Pandu. There are temples dedicated to Shiva, the Pandavas and Parusram. Hundreds of idols are believed to have been buried in the village. Often while digging or ploughing a farmer finds an idol or some old coins. A few years ago a farmer dug out a 4ft high, 3ft wide Shivlinga made of black stone. The village is virtually strewn with antiques. The Archaeological Survey of India has set up a godown in the village with officials to collect such finds of idols and inscriptions. Close by on a hill are two caves and a deep well. It is believed that the Pandavas spent their year of punishment in these caves and Bhim used to fill the well with water carried from the Yamuna to meet their daily requirements. Unfortunately no historian or archaeologist seems to have made any serious effort to excavate and examine the rich finds in the village. It is worth making a visit to this very interesting village. It can be completed in 2-3 hours from Kuan. From Naugaon the road turns north-west across the Yamuna river to Purola (1524m), an upcoming town, 19km on the banks of the Kamal river. This wide, fertile valley is called Kamal Sarai. Women in this valley have very pretty features. The men, by contrast, are not as spectacularly handsome! There is a rest house, tourist bungalow, some cheap hotels and several eating places at Purola. The road goes through tall pine forests to Jarmola, 10km, famous for apple orchards. Then it is downhill to Mori, 18km, and up again to Naitwar, 18km. The region beyond Naitwar up to Harkidoon has been designated a National Park where hunting is totally prohibited. A tourist is required to pay a camera and entry fee of about 30 rupees at Naitwar against a receipt which may be checked en route by the wardens. It is 12km from here to the bus terminus at Sankri (1800m). There is a tourist bungalow and 3-4 other guest-rooms. There are a few eating houses. Basic provisions are available in the shops. Hopefully the extension of the road to Taluka will be completed in a year or two. Porters are available at Sankri and almost every other village passed en route.

Day 1: The trek to Taluka overlooking the Supin river is 12km along an unfinished road through lush green forest. It is an almost level path taking an easy 5 hours. You get the first view of peaks in Harkidoon from here. Apart from tea houses, there is a forest bungalow and a tourist bungalow at Taluka (1900m). Basic provisions are available here as well as at Osla, the next and last village en route. There is a beautiful campsite beyond the forest rest house about an hour's partly downhill and then level walk at the junction of a stream and the Supin river. It is a lovely plateau from where the steep uphill climb to the village of Datmir starts. The old route to Osla went along the left bank of the Supin but most of the path has been washed away in a recent flood and the new route is through the village of Datmir. The main god worshipped by the people of the Tons valley is Mahashu. In a Mahashu temple at Anal village on the bank of the Tons, there are a number of statues of Shiva and Parvati, which adds weight to the theory that Mahashu is another name for Shiva. Mahashu is also worshipped by the people of Himachal and Jaunsar-Bhaber (in Dehra Dun district). The legend goes that Mahashu came from Kashmir to put an end to a ferocious demon who was harassing the people of these areas. A pious priest dreamt that Mahashu, one of four brothers in Kashmir, should be approached and requested to come to their rescue. Perhaps the legend simply gives some indication of migration from Kashmir to these places.

Day 2: The climb to Datmir village takes an hour. It is quite an interesting, big village with two shops but no tea houses! Most of the houses are two-storey with lavish use of wood. A narrow verandah encircles the house on three sides and is used to store dry grass for the animals in winter. It also functions as padding to protect the inner rooms from cold and winds. The ground floors have very low entrance doors. Each family usually has a separate wind-protected shed for cattle and a wooden granary called a 'Bhakar'. The Bhakar is about 6ft deep with 7 x 6ft partitioned storage space for different items. Very strong rat-proof wood is used for the granary, where grains, potatoes and other small items are stored. Some even store jewellery in it! It has a small window-like entrance with a lock on the door.

From Datmir it is another 15 minutes' ascent, then the path forks. Take the path to the left through terraced fields with a panoramic view of the Supin valley. It is level for about 4km, followed by 1km downhill to the village of Gangar, through a forest of chestnut, walnut, rhododendron and deodar. There is a tea house at Gangar and above it a temple. By now you are very close to the Supin river. Follow the path along the left bank towards Seema (Osla) (2559m). There is no suitable camping place but there is a forest rest house, a tourist bungalow and a tea house with two rooms for accommodation. The main village of Osla is 2km uphill across the river.

Polyandry is also practised in several villages of the Supin valley.

A groom has to pay a very heavy price for a bride, which can be anything from 8000 rupees. One of our porters had paid 30,000 rupees for his 17-year-old bride. In the practice of polyandry, the first child (irrespective of its father) becomes the child of the eldest brother, the second child becomes the child of the second brother, and so on. Divorces are very common and socially accepted by the villagers. Divorce is not a court procedure: the girl just walks out of her husband's house. When she remarries, the new husband has to reimburse the former husband the full amount paid by him to the girl's father, plus some more. Sometimes a girl has two, three or more husbands in succession and naturally her cost increases with each successive marriage!

Potatoes, beans, buckwheat and ramdana (Amaranthus Paniculatus), a fine white grain, grows in abundance in this valley. All these are cash crops, sold through contractors. They also rear sheep and goats and make their own woollen clothes. In winter young boys and girls assemble in a separate house after the evening meal to gossip, sing and dance. They are very hospitable and would offer guests some boiled potatoes with salt, and tea.

Day 3: Harkidoon is 9km from Osla and takes 6 hours. The path is across the bridge and straight uphill for 20 minutes. After the first climb it is almost level for 2km till you reach a section of big terraced fields and walnut trees. Remember not to take the lower path going down to the river. A gradual climb starts now, taking about 2 hours to Culcuttia dhar (ridge) with a lovely panorama of the Kalanag (6387m), Bandurpunch ranges and the forests surrounding Ruinsar lake, which begins to appear. Meadows open up after the Culcuttia dhar, which marks the end of the steep climb and the beginning of lush, green fields surrounded by conifer forest and rhododendrons in bloom during March and April. After about 2km the path descends for 20 minutes to the grass carpeted, broad valley. It is gradually uphill now for about $1^1/_2$ hours through meadow and forest to Harkidoon. A lovely campsite beside a stream provides panoramic views including the spectacular Swargarohini, right across the glacier. The Pandavas are believed to have gone to heaven (Swarg) through this peak. ('Arohan' means climb, hence the name Swargarohini.) There is a two-room forest rest house and a tourist bungalow. The rest house warden usually lives in Osla village. It is advisable to contact him through the forest rest house at Osla. We saw scented daphneys and rhododendron in bloom here in early May.

You can spend an enjoyable two days here without any ill effects from the altitude. The first day you could walk to the Jaundhar glacier, across meadow, in the direction of Swargarohini. On the second day a return trip to Borasu pass (about 4900m) is highly recommended. The path across this pass leads to Kinnor in Himachal Pradesh, which is a restricted area and not open to anyone without permission from the government. The trail follows the right bank of the stream in front of the forest rest house. It is a bit up and down for the first hour, across meadows and through rhododendron and juniper bushes, then gorgeous meadows appear one after the other, with the long ridge of Borasu pass and the inviting highest unnamed peak in the region (5890m) right ahead of you. It is very rare to have such a fantastic combination of gentle walking, grand close-up mountain views and spectacular meadow all in one day! The return journey to Osla takes an easy 4 hours, and a visit to the village and its temple is strongly recommended before heading back to the bungalow.

Extensions from Harkidoon

1. RUINSAR LAKE (3350m). GRADE C

If you do not wish to venture too high and wish to spend another two or three days in this fascinating region, a visit to Ruinsar lake at the foot of Mt. Kalanag would be good option, to view the peaks more closely. The lake is near the source of the Supin. The lake itself is not particularly attractive but the closer views of Mt. Kalanag and the Ruinsar ranges close by are superb. The lake can be reached in 8 hours from Osla. The route for the first 2km goes along the left bank of the Supin, then turns right up along the Ruinsar stream and through forest. Two nights are recommended at this place so that on the second day a return trip to Bali pass (4877m) could be made for a spectacular view of the Himalaya as far as the Gangotri range.

2. HARKIDOON-YAMUNOTRI VIA BALI PASS (4877m). GRADE C/D

This trek can be done from July to September when the snow on Bali pass has melted - you should be prepared for snow at any time on this route. You will need to be self-supporting on this trek for three days, with tents, provisions, kerosine oil, etc, and a guide from Osla village will be necessary. Before employing a guide or porter you must ensure that he knows the route. The trek provides extraordinary views and a variation whereby you can avoid repeating the Sankri-Taluka approach route and visit the Yamunotri shrine. The first day will take you on a gradual climb from Osla to above Ruinsar lake at about 4000m, through forest. The next day you cross the Bali pass and descend to the pastures of Damni (approx. 3400m). On the third day it is all the way downhill to Yamunotri, taking about 5 hours, and a further 5km downhill to Janki chatti for the night after visiting the temple.

3. OSLA-JANKICHATTI VIA TATKA/PULDHAR PASS (4580m). GRADE C/D

This trek is feasible from June to mid October. It is about the same difficulty as the Bali pass route but involves less high altitude with equally good views. A knowledgeable guide is a must. We nearly got lost on this trek with a local porter-cum-guide from Osla who persuaded us that he knew the way. You must be self-supporting, with tents, for three days. The route begins with a walk down from Osla to about half a kilometre short of Gangar village, then taking the narrow path uphill through terraced fields on your left. It is mostly uphill all day, first through terraced fields, followed by forest and finally through a meadow. Your first night will be at Tatka (3665m), about 9km, near shepherd huts, taking about 8 hours. On the second day continue uphill through meadows, across the Puldhar pass (3345m) and down to Puldhar. On the third day it is 6 hours' gradual downhill to Janki chatti. From there Yamunotri is a 6km trek and Hanuman chatti, the roadhead, is 7km.

4. OSLA-HANUMAN CHATTI VIA PHACHUKANDI PASS (4383m). GRADE C

This is a slightly easier trek with very good views. The pass can be crossed from mid May to mid October. An experienced guide is necessary and you must be self-supporting, including tents, for three days. The route for this traverse branches off from Taluka village uphill through the forest to Taloti bugyal on the first day. The second day crosses the Phachukandi pass and camp at Gujrat. The third day is to the Hanuman chatti bus stand.

Low Level Treks Near Mussoorie

If you do not have the time and resources to go deep into the Garhwal Himalaya for the more exhilarating treks, so can still enjoy the experience of 2-7 days' trekking around Mussoorie, with grand views of the Himalayan peaks. The routes are suggested below:

1. DEHRA DUN-DHANOLTI (2420m) AND SURKANDA DEVI TEMPLE (3030m). GRADE A

Best Season: March to mid June and mid September to mid December. There can be snow near Dhanolti in December. The trek is through villages and forests and provides stupendous views of the Garhwal

Himalaya including Mt. Swargarohini, Banderpunch, Gangotri ranges, Srikanth, Mt. Nandadevi, Bhrigupanth, Sumeru, Chaukhamba and Nilkanth. The trek does not involve any technical or high-altitude difficulty and can be done by any physically fit person without a guide. There may, however, be a difficulty in finding porters in Dehra Dun. You need to be self-supporting for meals for the first day and breakfast the next day.

Route: Take a 45 minute drive by taxi or bus from the local bus stand early in the morning to Sahastradhara (sulphur springs) (710m). Alternatively, get to Sahastradhara the night before and spend the night in the tourist bungalow or one of the simple hotels. This is a good picnic spot for a couple of hours. Bathing in the waters of the sulphur springs is believed to cure certain rheumatic diseases.

The first day's trek is to Naligaon (1525m). It takes 6 hours for this 9km trek on a mule path. It is used by milk-sellers travelling from the higher up villages to Sahastradhara. After about 2 hours the narrow uphill trail joins a nice broad path leading to Naligaon and the PPCL (Pyrites & Phosphates Chemicals Ltd) quarry. This broad path is through scented pine forest. There is a forest rest house in a picturesque spot below the road above Naligaon village. A permit for the bungalow should be obtained from the Divisional Forest Officer, Mussoorie, but it is not used frequently and the warden allows visitors to stay in it without a permit if it is free. The bungalow is connected by road to Dehra Dun via the Mussoorie bypass.

Next day continue the gradual ascent by road through pine forest, passing the PPCL workshop in about 2 hours and reaching the Mussoorie-Dhanolti road in a further hour. From there Dhanolti is 11km, taking 4 hours. Buranskanda provides commanding views of the valley below and the first spectacular view of the Gangotri range. It is 8km short of Dhanolti. Suddenly the wide Bhagirathi valley comes into view and in a still wider span appear dozens of peaks ranging from Banderpunch, Gangotri, to Badrinath. Outlined against the blue sky they seem to belong to another world. There are two tea houses providing a good excuse to gaze at the mountains while sipping tea. There is a lovely campsite below the road. The waterpoint is 2km further down the road. The forest consists of rhododendron, silver oak and deodar. In March-April rhododendrons will be in bloom and the oaks will have new pink leaves sprouting on the ends of the branches. Far below towards the Bhagirathi valley the hillsides are dotted with villages and terraced fields. Further down the road there are apple orchards for 25km up to Chamba. Dhanolti, in the middle of deodar forest, was a little hamlet until ten years ago. It has now become a popular tourist spot and is developing into a vegetable and potato supply centre for Dehra Dun and Delhi. There is a tourist bungalow, a couple of hotels and some eating places. The region is very popular with bird watchers. For views of the Himalaya you have to walk up about 100m to a state-run potato farm. There are lovely walks through the beautiful woods. From April onwards the flowers start appearing. You can spend an enjoyable 2-3 days here, making Dhanolti a base from which to walk around and enjoy the mountain panorama. A day return trip to Surkanda Devi temple, 18km, is possible from Dhanolti via Kaddukhal, 7km on the road to Chamba and Tehri. It is advisable to take a public bus to Kaddukhal and walk back. There are a few tea houses and a bungalow belonging to the Public Works Department at Kaddukhal. From here Surkanda is 2km uphill, taking just over an hour there and half an hour back. The mountain views from Surkanda are stupendous.

A three-day religious fair is held every year in May at Surkanda when hundreds of people from far and near visit the temple to offer prayers. According to legend, in prehistoric days a Yagya (religious ceremony) was being performed by King Dakshaprajapati, father of Parvati (Lord Shiva's consort). Shiva and Parvati were not invited to the Yagya. Parvati, however, attended it against Shiva's advice, and was not received well at her father's house. She felt deeply insulted and in anger jumped into the Havan Kund (sacred fire) before which the Yagya was being performed. The angry Shiva lifted her burnt body onto his Trident to take it away, but her head fell off at Surkanda and it became a holy place. It is believed that wishes are fulfilled if prayers are offered sincerely at this temple.

NEW TEHRI-CHAMBA-GAJA (Approx. 1570m)

If you have time, a visit to New Tehri town, 41km from Dhanolti, would be very interesting. Regular buses ply up to Chamba. You have to change at Chamba for the remaining 12km. New Tehri has been built to replace the old Tehri township on account of the Tehri Dam, currently being built, which will submerge nearly 80 villages, including Tehri, within two years. The town has been planned carefully, with all amenities. It commands a lovely view of the Himalaya as well as of the Tehri Dam. It will have hotels, facilities for boating and other water sports when the dam is complete.

There are low-altitude trekking possibilities in the New Tehri-Chamba-Gaja region, between 1500m and 2700m altitude. It is lovely unspoilt walking country. The walks are through whispering forests of deodar, pine, oak and rhododendron. One of the recommended treks is in the area surrounding Dandachali. It is important to take a tent on this trek, but simple meals can be had in the tea houses and roadside eating places. It is an easy 'A' grade trek.

The route: Arrive Chamba (1534m) the night before from Rishikesh, Dehra Dun, Mussoorie or Dhanolti. There is a tourist bungalow and some simple hotels for accommodation and meals. From Chamba itself there are good mountain views. Next morning take a bus to Chaunrikhal, 8km, on the road to New Tehri. From here there is a road to Dandachali, another 8km, but it would be more enjoyable to walk to Dandachali, taking about 3 hours and passing en route the Panthnagar Agricultural University campus. It is a quiet route through forest with good views of the valley below as well as the Himalaya. Dandachali, with a good campsite, is approximately 1830m altitude in the middle of a pine forest. In the afternoon follow the path across the campsite leading to some huts on a ridge through pine forest about 200m higher. From the ridge there are lovely views of the Garhwal Himalaya. The villagers are very friendly and helpful. In the evening return to Dandachali for the night - a 3 hour return journey in all. Next morning follow the path along the ridge opposite the tea houses. Continue walking along the ridge through the lovely forest towards Digothi village. A few shepherd huts are passed on the way, ending up at a huge water storage tank that has never been used because of defective workmanship. A further 15 minutes down the ridge is a temple with fabulous views of the Garhwal Himalaya and the entire Tehri Garhwal covering Rishikesh-Mussoorie-Dhanolti-Pratap Nagar and the Bhagirathi valley and culminating with the source of the Ganges. You can return to Chamba in the afternoon.

TREK TO NAGTIBBA (3048m). GRADE B

Best season: March to mid June and October to end of November.

Nagtibba (the mountain of the snake god) is north-east of Mussoorie with excellent views of the Garhwal Himalaya ranging over 250km, commencing with the Swargarohini ranges and ending with graceful Nandadevi. This lovely short trek is interesting for bird watchers and nature lovers. Tents and provisions must be carried.

Approach route: The trek starts from Dhanolti but porters must be picked up at Mussoorie. The drive from Dehra Dun to Dhanolti takes $2^1/2$ hours. You should aim to arrive at Dhanolti by 0800 and, given some time to organise loads for porters, be able to leave by 0900. Walk along the path towards Kaddukhal for about half a kilometre and take the first lower mule track to your left. It is a lovely easy path through forest. After a while villages start appearing below the path.

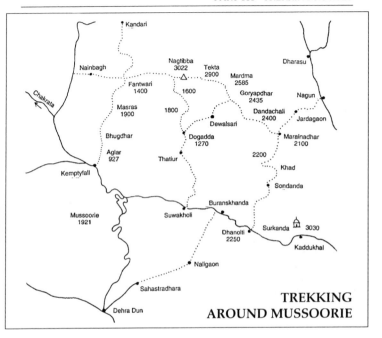

TREKKING AROUND MUSSOORIE

Sondanda is crossed in 3 hours. From there Khad (2430m), 5km, taking another 3 hours maximum, will be your camp for the first night. Leaving the village next day, a good path on your left continues to Marainadhar for about an hour, with good birdlife, and views of the Gangotri range and the valley below. Then it is gradually uphill through forest for about 5 hours to the Bagi Bhainswar huts. The uphill path continues for half an hour. The climb is duly compensated by excellent views. It is now much easier for $2^{1}/_{2}$ hours up to the summer village of Dhancholi via Birthat. The final 20 minutes is steep uphill. Camp should be made in the oak forest above the village. On the third day the path descends through forest for 1km then is reasonably level for about 6km to Goryapdhar. A further 2km on is a lovely camping ground. Goryapdhar can also be reached on foot from Thatyur, 13km, which is connected by road (about 2 hours' drive). There are some Gujjar and shepherd huts here, surrounded by thick forest. The path goes uphill about 200m through a maple and oak forest, taking an hour. Then it is gradually uphill for 2km till you

183

meet a ridge leading to the Madma huts at about 2790m. It will take 7 hours to do 13km today. Excellent mountain views can be had of Bandarpunch, the Gangotri ranges and Mt. Trishul and Nandaghunti, covering over 200km of panorama.

On the fourth day take a gradual 200m descent down the ridge to Paunth, enjoying the grand mountain panorama the whole day. At a shepherd hut a path forks down to the big prosperous village of Ontar. A further climb through forest to Tekta (2900m) takes 2 hours. Nagtibba is half an hour's walk further along the ridge. There is no water available on this ridge so you should carry a packed lunch and water. Camp for the night about $1^{1/2}$km downhill on the other side at a lovely campsite near a dilapidated forest bungalow with plenty of water. A religious festival is held here at the Nag temple in May each year.

The next day is 6km to Bhandsar on a steep downhill cattle path and in a further 3 hours you reach Nainbagh on the road to Mussoorie, a 2 hour drive. This region is called Jaunsar. They love singing and dancing here and it would be interesting to spend a night in one of the villages.

Appendixes

PEAKS OPEN IN GARHWAL FOR CLIMBING
WITH PERMISSION FROM IMF:

Name of Peak	Height	Longitude	Latitude	
Swargarohini-I	6252m	78° 31'	31° 06'	
Swargarohini-II	6248m	"	"	
Unnamed Peak				
(West of Swargarohini)	6247m	78° 30'	30° 06'	
"	6209m	"	"	
Unnamed peak				
(East of Swargarohini)	5654m	78° 35'	31° 04'	
"	5873m	"	"	
"	5736m	"	"	
Unnamed peak				
(North of Banderpunch)	5791m	78° 34'	31° 04'	
Ruinsara	5487m			
Bara Sukha	5530m			
Black peak (Kalanag)	6387m	78° 34'	31° 02'	
White peak	6103m			
Banderpunch	6302m	78° 33'	31° 00'	
Banderpunch (west)	6102m	78° 31'	"	
Unnamed peak	5800m	78° 37'	"	
Srikanta	6133m	78° 48'	30° 57'	
Unnamed peak				
(west of Srikanta)	5544m	78° 47'	30° 57'	
Unnamed peak				
(East south of Srikanta)	6023m	78° 49'	"	
Rudugaira	5819m	78° 52'	30° 56'	
Gangotri-I	6672m	78° 51'	30° 55'	
Gangotri-II	6590m	78° 51'	30° 54'	
Gangotri-III	6577m	78° 52'	30° 53'	
Joanli	6632m	78° 51'	30° 51'	
Unnamed peak	5834m	78° 50'	30° 52'	
Unnamed peak	6038m	"	"	
Unnamed peak	5975m	78° 53'	36° 56'	

PEAKS IN KEDARGANGA VALLEY

Jogin-I	6456m	78° 56'	30° 53'	
Jogin-II	6342m	78° 56'	30° 54'	
Jogin-III	6116m	"	"	
Thaley sagar	6904m	78° 59'	30° 52'	
Bhrigupanth	6772m	79° 00'	30° 53'	

Name of Peak	Height	Longitude	Latitude
Unnamed peak			
(North of Bhrigupanth)	6529m	79° 01'	30° 55'
"	6568m	79° 00'	30° 57'
"	6508m	78° 90'	30° 57'
Manda	6511m	78° 51'	30° 52'
Manda-II	6567m	79° 00'	30° 55'
Bhrigu Parbat	6000m	78° 59'	30° 57'
" (west)	5944m	"	"
Hanuman peak	5366m	"	30° 58'
Unnamed peak			
(Meru Bamak)	6044m	79° 01'	30° 53'
Meru	6660m	79° 02'	30° 52'
Meru North	6450m	"	30° 53'
Meru East	6261m	79° 01'	"
Unnamed peak	6602m	79° 02'	"
KIRTI BAMAK			
Kirti Stambh	6270m	79° 01'	30° 49'
Unnamed peak			
(north of Kirti Stambh)	6123m	"	30° 50'
Kirti Stambh-I	6274m	"	30° 49'
Kirti Stambh-II	6259m	"	30° 50'
Bhartekunta	6578m	79° 02'	30° 48'
GANGOTRI GLACIER			
Kedarnath	6968m	79° 04'	30° 48'
Kedarnath Dome	6830m	"	30° 44'
Mahalaya Parbat	5970m		
Unnamed Peak			
(south-east of Kedarnath)	6443m	"	30° 47'
Burma Gupha	5892m	79° 05'	30° 48'
Sumeru Parbat	6350m	79° 08'	30° 46'
Kharcha Kund	6632m	"	30° 47'
Shivling	6543m	79° 04'	30° 53'
Shivling-II	6505m	79° 05'	"
Baby Shivling	5606m		
Bhagirathi-I	6856m	79° 09'	30° 51'
Bhagirathi-II	6512m	79° 08'	30° 53'
Bhagirathi-III	6454m	"	30° 52'
Unnamed peak (south-east			
of Bhagirathi II)	6193m	79° 09'	30° 51'
"	6477m	79° 10'	30° 50'
"	6504m	79° 09'	30° 40'
Vasuki Parbat	6792m	79° 10'	30° 53'

Name of Peak	Height	Longitude	Latitude
Unnamed peak (South of Vasuki Parbat)	6702m	"	30° 52'
Satopanth	7075m	"	30° 51'
Unnamed peak (North of Satopanth)	6008m	"	30° 52'
CHATURANGI BAMAK			
Chaturangi	6304m	79° 11'	30° 56'
Unnamed peak	5993m	79° 12'	"
Unnamed peak (east of Chaturangi)	6180m	79° 09'	"
Unnamed peak	6210m	79° 12'	30° 55'
Sudarshan Parbat	6507m	79° 06'	30° 59'
Unnamed peak (south of Sudarshan)	6166m	"	30° 58'
Unnamed peak (south-west of Sudarshan)	6002m	79° 05'	"
North of Sudarshan	6341m	79° 06'	30° 60'
Thelu	6000m		
Koteshwar	6035m		
Chatarbhuj	6655m		

The following peaks on the rim of the Nandadevi Basin may also be attempted by routes from outside the Nandadevi Sanctuary:

Nandakhat	6545m	79° 58'	30° 18'
Panwali Dwar	6663m	79° 57'	30° 17'
Mrigthuni	6855m	79° 50'	"
Trishul-I	7120m	79° 47'	30° 19'
Trishul-II	6690m	"	30° 18'
Trishul-III	6008m	79° 46'	30° 15'
Tharkot	6099m		
Nandaghunti	6390m		
Ronti	6063m		
Bhanoti	5645m		
Baljuari	5922m		
Nandakot	6861m		
Nanda Bhanar	6350m	79° 48'	30° 20'

APPENDIX B

APPLICATION FOR CLIMBING PEAKS IN THE
INDIAN HIMALAYA BY FOREIGNERS (To be submitted in triplicate)

a)   Paragraph 11 (a) of the Foreigners Order 1948, issued vide Government of India, Ministry of Home Affairs, Notification No. 11013/4/78-F.I dated 9.1.1979, provides that notwithstanding anything contained in the Foreigners (Exemption) Order, 1957, no foreigner or group of foreigners shall climb any mountain peak in India without obtaining the prior permission in writing of the Central Government on an application made in that behalf through the Indian Mountaineering Foundation and without complying with such conditions including specification of route to be followed, accompaniment by a Liaison Officer, use of photographic and wireless communication equipment as may be laid down in this behalf, section 14 of the Foreigners Act, 1946, further provides that: "If any person contravenes the provisions of this Act or of any Order made there under, or any direction given in pursuance of this Act or such Order, he shall be punished with punishment for a term which may extend to five years and shall be liable to fine, and if such person has entered into a bond in pursuance of clause (f) of subsection (2) of section (3), his bond shall be forfeited, and any person bound thereby shall pay the penalty thereof, or show cause to the satisfaction of the convicting court why such penalty should not be paid."

b)   If any particulars required in the Application Form are not furnished, the case will not be processed.

Part I

1)   Name and height of the peak/peaks to be climbed with coordinates, if possible. (Alternative peaks may be suggested in case the peak/peaks is/are already booked for another expedition.)

2)   A rough route chart of the peak/peaks clearly indicating which face/ridge is proposed to be attempted. (seven copies)

3)   Duration of the expedition and approximate dates of arrival in and departure from India.

3A) Actual climbing period. (Base camp to peak and back to base camp)

4)   A list of members (including the leader) showing the names, father's name, permanent address, age with date of birth, nationality, mountaineering training and experience, occupation, passport number, date and place of issue, and next of kin, with addresses (seven copies), together with a passport-sized photograph of each member. In case all the particulars are not handy at the time of submission of the application, the names of the members, parentage and number and date of passport may be enclosed (seven copies). Remaining particulars must be sent later. Indicate if any member is or has been a member of the Armed Forces or the Diplomatic Corps.

5)   Source of financing the expedition in broad terms.

6) Date of application submitted to the Indian Embassy for 'entry visa'. (Tourist visa or Transit visa will not entitle a person to join an expedition to the Indian Himalaya. Application for conversion of such visas after arrival in India is not normally entertained.) The name and place of the Indian Mission which should be authorised to issue visas may be indicated.

7) Whether walkie-talkie sets or other similar equipment will be brought to India. If so, the enclosed application form should be filled in and attached (in triplicate). (*Author's note:* The application form should be obtained from IMF.)

8) Whether radio weather broadcasts may be arranged.

9) Two copies of complete lists of mountaineering equipment, clothing, foodstuff etc. to be brought to India should be attached showing approximate weight and C.I.F. value of consumable and non-consumable items in separate lists.

Signature of the leader

Undertaking
I undertake

i)   That the goods except such of the consumable stores as may be consumed or other articles as may be lost or left on the mountains, shall be re-exported within six months from the date of importation.

ii) In the event of failure to do so duty which would have been levied on such goods, but for the exemption, shall be paid.

iii) I hereby undertake that,
   a) I will not damage, or destroy any vegetation or burn or allow to be burnt any juniper or other plants in the mountainous areas which we visit. We will further carry adequate supply of kerosene or other fuel.
   b) It will also be ensured that the porters accompanying the expedition will observe the same conditions.
   c) Action will be taken by me to ensure that the mountain environment will be cleared by burying/burning the garbage at various camps.

iv) That in the event of requisitioning helicopter for evacuation, the charges for helicopter sorties and subsequent hospitalisation will be fully paid to the Indian Mountaineering Foundation on presentation of bills.

v)   I shall also ensure that the Liaison Officer is treated as a member of the expedition and adequately equipped as per our own standard and that his requirement of proper food/porter, etc. be fully met.

vi) I have noted the above instructions and shall comply with them.

vii) That I shall submit to the Indian Mountaineering Foundation a report on the expedition immediately on its expiry and the photographs within two months.

Date: Signature of the leader
                                                      (Name in Full)

APPENDIX C
INSTRUCTIONS FOR FOREIGN EXPEDITIONS
Part II

1. It will speed up processing of a proposal if applications along with required documents are sent to the Indian Mountaineering Foundation, Benito Jurea Road, Anand Niketan, New Delhi-110021, at least six months before the proposed date of arrival of an expedition in India. If the name of the ports of disembarkation and names of members and their passport numbers are not received at least three months before the date of arrival of a team, granting of the Mountaineering Visa may be delayed and the team may have to wait in their own country or in New Delhi.

2. Members of the expedition are advised:
    i) To get themselves medically examined before starting on the journey, if there is the slightest doubt about their fitness;
    ii) To ensure that at least one or two of the members of the expedition have experience of high altitude climbing in the Himalaya;
    iii) To bring wireless sets with them for communication between camps on the mountain and the base camp;
    iv) To bring radio receiving sets in case weather forecasts of the All India Radio are required to be arranged by the IMF which is desirable especially for climbing difficult peaks; and
    v) To study the booklet *While in the Himalayas, dos & donts* a copy of which can be purchased from the IMF office on payment.

3. Every foreign expedition has to be accompanied by an Indian Liaison Officer, who is a mountaineer. He is to be treated as a member of the expedition team and provided with equipment/clothing of the same standard as provided to the other members. An expedition will not be allowed to start for the mountain if the Liaison Officer's equipment is not brought and is not of the same standard as for other members. The cost of the Liaison Officer's transport, one cook-cum-porter (from the roadhead), board and lodging from Delhi to the mountains and back will be borne by the expedition. The standard of board and lodging of the Liaison Officer should also be the same as for other members of the expedition. If any imported food is carried, the expedition should bring a substitute for beef which is not liked by most Indian Liaison Officers. The pay and allowances of the Liaison Officer are met by their employers in India for the duration of the expedition and the cost of reaching New Delhi and going back to his or her place of residence is not the liability of the expedition.

4. A Liaison Officer has to accompany each foreign expedition irrespective of whether the peak lies in the restricted area or open area. If the exact date of a team in New Delhi and mode of travel are not intimated at least two months before the date of arrival in India, the team may have to wait in New Delhi for the Liaison Officer who usually comes from an outstation.

5. A Liaison Officer helps in hiring porters, mules, booking accommodation on the way to the mountains, hiring transport from New Delhi to roadhead

and back, maintaining liaison with the local civil and military authorities and the Indian Mountaineering Foundation in case of illness or accident of members while on the mountains. The Liaison Officer is also expected to climb to upper camps and even summit according to his experience and competence. The Liaison Officer may be expected to carry a load of between 10-15kg on the approach walk.

6. On arrival at the last District or Sub-Division of Garhwal, Himachal Pradesh or Jammu & Kashmir, the leader and the Liaison Officer must report to the District Magistrate/Deputy Commissioner or the Sub-Divisional Magistrate. Expeditions are advised not to engage porters by direct negotiation with them. The District authorities will endeavour to help in engaging porters for the expedition at the prescribed rates.

7. As soon as a proposal is received from the expedition, the Indian Mountaineering Foundation will book the peak(s) provisionally, subject to the availability of the peak(s) and inform the party. (Permission from the Government of India to climb is essential and the Indian Mountaineering Foundation will take steps to obtain this permission on receipt of application form with full particulars and documents.) On receipt of intimation of provisional booking, the party should send the booking fee (together with the completed application form) at the following rates (*author's note:* please **re-check with IMF** on latest rules and rates):

Height of Peak   **Rate of booking fee payable** (Revised w.e.f. 1.1.1991)

Height of Peak	Rate		
Below 6000m	US$ 600		
Between 6001m to 6500m	US$ 900	For peaks Nun and Kun in	
Between 6501m to 7000m	US$ 1350	Kashmir Himalaya	US$ 2250
7001m and above	US$ 1800	For peaks in Karakorams	US$ 3000

If the booking fee is not received within two months from the date of issue of the IMF intimation, the provisional booking will be cancelled and the peak(s) offered to the next party on the waiting list. The fee in US$ only should be remitted by a bank draft on a bank in New Delhi in favour of the Indian Mountaineering Foundation. No cheques will be entertained. In the event of the cancellation of the expedition after booking, 25% of the booking fee will be forfeited. No unbooked peaks should be climbed even as a part of acclimatisation.

If, after proceeding to and attempting the peak for which permission has been obtained, the expedition desires to attempt an additional peak, it shall make such a request in writing to the Liaison Officer who will allow such an attempt provided that the said additional peak is free from other expeditions. A booking fee is payable for such additional peak at 50% of the normal fee, but the attempt/climb should be within 45 days.

8. In the event of fatal accident to a porter or a high altitude porter, compensation will be payable by the expedition team at the rate of Rs.10,000 and Rs.15,000 per porter respectively. Compensation for partial injury will be decided by the IMF in consultation with the leader. Expeditions are advised to insure the porters, especially the high altitude porters, on

payment of a small amount on arrival in India at a premium which will cover both death and injury.

9.   The Liaison Officer will be insured by the IMF for Rs.100,000 before he leaves for the mountains. The members of the expedition are advised to get insurance cover for themselves in their own countries.

10.   In the event of any accident, while on the mountains, arrangement is made for evacuation of a casualty by helicopter to the nearest hospital, charges for which are of the order of Rs.25,000 or above for each helicopter sortie, depending upon the flight time etc. The charges are to be borne by the expedition. It is therefore advisable that the insurance of the members includes accident risks.

11.   A detailed report in the prescribed form is to be submitted to the IMF (with photographs and route map) after the expedition is over. It should specifically mention how many porters were recruited from what source and what payment was made to the porter per day, per head and whether any difficulty was experienced in recruiting them or with any persons in India.

12.   I have read the above instructions and I agree to abide by them.

Place: Signature of the leader
Date: (Name in full)

BIBLIOGRAPHY

FLORA

Polunin, O & Stainton, A.   (1984 & later reprints) *Flowers of the Himalaya*. OxfordUniversity Press.ISBN 0 19 2176234 pp580

Stainton, A. (1988) *Flowers of the Himalaya, a supplement*. OUP. ISBN 0 19 561981.1 pp86

Bole, P.V. & Yogini, V. (1986) *Field Guide to the Common Trees of India*. Bombay. OUP.

FAUNA

Salim, A. & Ripley, S.D. (1995 (2nd edn)) *A Pictorial Guide to the Birds of the Indian Subcontinent*. Bombay Natural History Soc.ISBN 0 19 5616340 106 plates by John Henry Dick depicting 1241 spp.This is the most useful field guide to the birds of India, reproducing the plates from the Compact Edition without the text.

Salim, A. & Ripley, S.D. (1987)*Compact Handbook of the Birds of India and Pakistan*. OUP. ISBN 19 5620631 104 plates by John Henry Dick pp820
This is the best single volume guide to the birds of India but is far too weighty for use in the field.

Prater, S.H. (1971)*The Book of Indian Animals*. Bombay Natural History Soc. OUP. ISBN 0 19 5621697 pp324

Daniel, J.C. (1983)*The book of Indian Reptiles*. Bombay Natural History Soc. OUP. ISBN 0 19 5621689 pp141